THE WINTER TABLE

LISA LEMKE

·FIRESIDE FEASTS·
FOR FAMILY AND FRIENDS

STERLING EPICURE
New York

STERLING EPICURE
New York

An Imprint of Sterling Publishing Co., Inc.
1166 Avenue of the Americas
New York, NY 10036

This 2017 edition published by Sterling Publishing Co., Inc.
Portions of this book were first published in Sweden in 2013 as *Allt I En Gryta*
and in 2015 as *Lisa På Landet* by Bonnier Fakta.

ISBN 978-1-4549-2254-4

Distributed in Canada by Sterling Publishing Co., Inc.
c/o Canadian Manda Group, 664 Annette Street
Toronto, Ontario, Canada M6S 2C8
Distributed in the United Kingdom by GMC Distribution Services
Castle Place, 166 High Street, Lewes, East Sussex, England BN7 1XU
Distributed in Australia by NewSouth Books
45 Beach Street, Coogee, NSW 2034, Australia

For information about custom editions, special sales, and premium and corporate purchases,
please contact Sterling Special Sales at 800-805-5489 or specialsales@sterlingpublishing.com.

Manufactured in China

2 4 6 8 10 9 7 5 3 1

sterlingpublishing.com

CONTENTS

INTRODUCTION

FOOD FOR THE HEART AND SOUL

When there's a nip in the air and the first snowflakes fly, the desire to move closer to the hearth inspires a shift in what we eat—and enjoy—to feel comforted and sustained. And is there anything more satisfying than sharing a delicious, hearty meal with family and friends in a cozy, warm kitchen or by the fireplace?

I'm from Sweden, where there's plenty of cold weather and a lot of creativity in making winter dishes that are not only sustaining but also that excite the palate with both traditional flavors and styles of preparation, as well as borrowed ingredients, textures, and accents from other cultures. None of this has to eat up all of your time in the kitchen! I love dishes that I can put together quickly—especially if it means I can just throw everything into a single pot, whether it's a casserole, a saucepan, a Dutch oven, or an old (but well-loved) cast iron frying pan. For me, that's comfort food at its best. Relaxing, simple, and rustic, so that you can devote time to something else—like unwinding and enjoying the season.

In all the world's cuisines, cooks love and often rely on one-pot dishes—in some places because there's only a single fire to cook on, and in others, because it saves time and there's a battle every day over who will do the dishes. No matter what the circumstances, it is a lovely convenience to simply let all the ingredients in a dish just simmer away on the stove or in the oven—in a single pot!

With a little planning, these recipes can provide shortcuts to amazingly quick meals and treats, as well as to sumptuously slow-cooked ones. Whether it's fried rice, tarragon chicken cooked in white wine, or chocolate sauce, no one will be able to resist.

Regardless of where you are during the colder months of the year, you can stock your pantry and fridge with wonderful things to make everyone feel happy, satisfied, and relaxed. With this cookbook I hope to slow down the tempo a bit and to let in the warmth. No matter how simple the meal, if it is cooked from the heart and enjoyed with the people you love, it will inspire happy memories, a powerful feeling of connection, and yes, it will all taste pretty amazing, too!

Dig in!

Lisa

TOOLS & TIPS

Love relationships and the pots and pans you use have a lot in common: Be extra choosy and nurture them carefully, and both your relationships and your cookware can last a long time. Who wants to buy new pots every fifteen minutes? Besides, I'd rather use a few really good ones, instead of a bunch of flashy, expensive pans that don't really do the job. Quality always wins over appearance!

Two cast iron pans in different sizes will cover most of your frying and slow-cooking needs. In the best of all worlds, one pan would be both wide enough and deep enough to accommodate all-in-one recipes; the other pan can be shallower, with sloping sides so that it is easier to flip pancakes, omelets, and the like.

Speaking of essentials, a big, lidded stockpot is a must to have on hand for making soups and boiling pasta, as well as two or three saucepans in different sizes for cooking a couple of cups of rice or anything else to boiling an egg or two or making a simple sauce.

And, of course, you need a roasting pan that's big enough to prepare everything from a large roast to enough lasagna to feed everyone on your street.

And that large, heavy-gauge stockpot with a tight-fitting lid will do a variety of jobs. In addition to soup-making and poaching, it can hold steamer inserts of various sizes (happily, they're inexpensive and easy to find) for vegetables, fish, dumplings, and more.

What about casseroles? A deep, heavy-bottomed enameled cast iron pot like a Dutch oven, with a cover that fits snugly, is ideal for slow-cooking stews, soups, and all sorts of hearty winter meals. There's no need to run out and buy a brand new Dutch oven or heavy cast iron pot if your budget is tight. It's surprising what you can find in yard sales and flea markets, and you can always resurrect your grandma's cast iron pots and pans. All they need is a little conditioning and TLC, and you're good to go.

I also recommend having an oval, enameled cast iron gratin dish on hand, ideally with a cover, as well as a set of sturdy, oven-safe baking dishes.

CAST IRON TLC

A little tender loving care prolongs the life of your cast iron skillet and guarantees better results when you use it. A pan with untreated casting, *i.e.* casting that is not enameled, will easily start to rust if you

don't take care of it correctly. To do this you need to season your skillet. Start by scrubbing it in warm, soapy water. Dry it thoroughly and then spread the inside of the pan, as well as the handle, with plenty of vegetable oil. Put the skillet in the oven and turn up the heat to about 375°F (190°C) for 1 hour or so. Remove the pan from the oven and let it cool down. Use paper towels to wipe off the oil. You're now ready to start cooking! To be on the safe side, use a little extra oil. You can always drain it off, if your dish doesn't require all of the oil, and your skillet will thank you.

What about cleaning cast iron? Never use detergent! Instead, wash your pot or pan by hand (never in the dishwasher) with hot water and a sponge or stiff brush. Wash it when the pan is still hot, so it's easier to clean. But be careful never to use cold water on a hot cast iron pan—it can actually break. Dry it immediately with paper towels or in the stove, if it's still warm. Using a paper towel, cover the inside of the skillet (and the outside as well, if you like) with a very light coating of vegetable oil. Dry off any excess oil and store the skillet in a dry place. If you still get rust in your pan, just reseason it by *gently* scrubbing the inside with a steel brush and wiping off the rust. Pour some cooking oil into the pan and rub it around to cover the interior. Put the pan in the oven for 2–3 hours at 300°F (150°C). When it has cooled down, wipe off the oil, and your cast iron pan is as good as new!

SELECTING MEAT FOR SLOW-COOKING AND MAKING BROTH FROM BONES

We consumers are extremely fillet-driven when it comes to preparing meat, and often forget that there are lots of other amazing cuts of beef, pork, and lamb to use. And though it might take little longer to fry or slow-cook them, these cuts are just as fabulous. I'm thinking of beef short ribs, chuck, and pot roast, pork shoulder, lamb shanks, and much more. These cuts are also budget-friendly— not the least because you can use the bones to make excellent stocks and broths. Just toss the bones into a large stockpot (about 6 quarts), add some onion, garlic, carrots, celery root, maybe a little tomato paste, and herbs, and pour in plenty of water to cover the bones and vegetables. Put the lid on the pot and bring the mixture to a gentle boil. Then reduce the heat to a very low simmer and cook, with the lid slightly ajar, for 4–5 hours or longer, adding more water, if necessary to keep the bones and veggies submerged. The stock becomes more flavorful the longer you simmer it. Skim off any fat, skin, or foam that rises to the top.

Let the broth cool and then refrigerate it. Remove any fat that may have solidified on top of the stock. You can now freeze the soup in small portions and use it later. This is about as simple and as good as it gets!

FIVE TIPS FOR MAKING GREAT ONE-POT MEALS

1. Allow meat to come to room temperature before you brown it in a hot pan. Do not fry too much meat in the pan at one time, because that will lower the temperature, and the meat will start cook through instead of browning. Instead, carefully brown a little meat at a time.

2. When you are cooking all-in-one dishes like stews, soups, and oven-baked casseroles, add salt early on and then add a bit more, to taste, when the dish is fully cooked. With spices: add some in the beginning then even more at the end. Doing so will yield more complex flavors.

3. If you have time, prepare the dish a day in advance and let it rest in the refrigerator overnight. It will do wonders for the taste and consistency.

4. Onions are truly the secret ingredients that make this type of cooking so delicious, especially recipes that take a little longer to prepare. With enough time and heat, onions become sweet and give body and roundness to a dish. So give onions a chance, even if you don't normally appreciate them. Who knows—you might just surprise yourself!

5. Don't forget that a well-seasoned cast iron pot with a secure lid works just as well for slow-cooking in the oven as it does on your stovetop.

SEASONING

It bears repeating: always season your cooking in two phases, once at the beginning of cooking, and then at the end, before serving. Spices that are added initially lose their intensity during cooking, but contribute great flavor, nonetheless. Spices that are added at the end of the cooking time add a burst of flavor that can elevate a dish from good to great. And some spices, like curry mixtures, cumin, and saffron need to be heated for their unique flavors to blossom.

If you are using a blend of spices and herbs to flavor a dish, bundle them together in a cheesecloth sachet, tied shut with a piece of kitchen string, before you toss them into the pot and start cooking; that way, it will be easy to remove loose spices and herbs just before serving. You don't want your guests to end up chewing on a tough piece of bay leaf or allspice instead of enjoying their meal.

ONE-POT WINTER WONDERS

Lamb Tagine, 4

Veggie Curry with Chickpeas, 7

Red Beet Stew with Caraway and Goat Cheese, 8

Italian Chicken Stew, 11

Venison Goulash with Apples and Horseradish, 12

Beef Stew with Fennel, Porter, and Chocolate, 15

Root Veggie Stew, 16

Hearty Chicken Stew, 19

Pulled Pork with BBQ Sauce, 20

Chuck Steak Chili, 23

Julia Child's Coq au Vin, 24

Doesn't it feel a bit like witchcraft to cook in a pot? You toss in all the ingredients, including plenty of spices, and cover it with a lid. A couple of hours later, everything has been transformed into a fantastic potion filled with flavor.

One of the things I like best about one-pot dishes is that they almost always taste better after they've had a chance to rest in the fridge for a day or two. The recipes in this chapter are eclectic, ranging from venison goulash and a lamb tagine to pulled pork and coq au vin. It also includes some delicious vegetable stews. I love to make these in the wintertime, when everyone craves something hearty and soul satisfying to eat—and they're just as easy to make, and always welcome around the table, in the fall or spring—anytime, really. I hope these recipes make you love one-pots as much as I do!

LAMB TAGINE

The aromatic spices, sweet fruit, and spicy lamb in this dish will take you on a superb culinary journey across the Straits of Gibraltar to North Africa, right onto your plate. A tagine is an earthenware casserole with a conical lid that is essential to North African cuisine, but you don't have to have one of these marvelous pots to make this dish—a regular saucepan with a lid will do just as well. If you have the time, cook this dish a day in advance—the flavors ripen and get even better.

20 minutes + 1½ hours ▪ 4 servings

2 large yellow onions

3 cloves garlic

1⅓ pounds (600g) boneless lamb meat

2 tablespoons butter

1½ tablespoons ground coriander seeds

1 teaspoon freshly ground cardamom

3 teaspoons harissa paste (see note)

1½–2 teaspoons salt

5 ounces (150g, about ¾ cup) dried apricots

½ cup (1 dl raisins)

3⅓–3¾ cups (8–9dl) beef, lamb, or veal broth

3 tablespoons tomato paste

Freshly ground black pepper

Handful of parsley, chopped, for garnish

1. Peel and chop the onion and garlic coarsely. Cut the meat into ¾-inch (2cm) cubes.

2. Melt the butter in a large pot or saucepan and brown the meat with the coriander seeds, cardamom, and harissa paste. Add the onion and garlic and sauté until soft. Add the salt, apricots, raisins, broth, and tomato paste.

3. Bring the mixture to a boil, skim, and let it simmer with the lid on for about 1½ hours or until the meat is tender. Add more liquid, if needed, while the mixture is simmering. Season with plenty of black pepper and garnish with chopped parsley. Serve with couscous.

NOTE Harissa, a popular North African spice paste, is made from dried chiles, garlic, tomato paste, preserved lemon, fresh cilantro, and spices such as coriander, cumin, caraway, paprika, and cayenne. Harissa is usually sold in a can or jar and will last for 2–3 weeks in the refrigerator. You can buy harissa at most specialty stores these days, and even in some supermarkets, where you'll find it stocked with Sriracha and other spicy and hot sauces and condiments.

VEGGIE CURRY
WITH
CHICKPEAS

Hold on to your hat—this will be spicy! Vindaloo curry gives a nice aromatic kick to the chick-peas and coconut milk, but for the slightly more fainthearted, you can replace half the vindaloo with either regular yellow curry or tandoori.

10 minutes + 25 minutes ■ 4 servings

2–3 tablespoons butter

2 large cloves garlic

½ leek

1½ tablespoons spicy curry powder, such as vindaloo curry

2-inch piece (25g) fresh ginger

2 medium (200g) carrots

1 14-ounce can (400g) chickpeas, rinsed and drained

1 14-ounce can (400dl) coconut milk

¾ cup (2dl) vegetable broth

8 ounces (250g, ¼ head) cauliflower

Salt and black pepper

Chopped almonds (for garnish)

Fresh cilantro (for garnish)

1. Peel and finely chop the garlic. Slice and then rinse the leek carefully to get rid of any sand or grit. Finely chop the ginger (see peeling tips on page 68). Peel and cut the carrots into thick slices. Break the florets off the cauliflower and cut the stalk into small pieces.

2. Melt the butter in a large pot or saucepan and sauté the garlic, leek, and curry powder until the onion is soft. Stir while sautéing. Add the ginger, carrots, and chickpeas, and cook for another short while. Stir in coconut milk and broth and bring the mixture to a boil.

3. Simmer the mixture covered, for about 15 minutes. Add the cauliflower and cook for 5–10 minutes more or until the cauliflower is soft. Season the curry with salt and pepper, and sprinkle the almonds and fresh cilantro over the top. If you like, serve the dish with Basmati rice and naan or papadums.

Cauliflower is a fantastic vegetable, but don't cook it too long. Otherwise it will become dull and mushy, and that won't make anyone happy.

RED BEET STEW
WITH
CARAWAY AND GOAT CHEESE

Even though there are few things that I love more than chewing on juicy ribs or diving into a plate of homemade sausages, I think it is inspiring to cook greener dishes, where meat is added for flavor more than anything else. For me, that's the future. Here, I have taken autumn's sweetest and most beautiful beets and cooked them in an earthy casserole topped with creamy goat cheese.

15 minutes + 45 minutes ▪ 4 servings

1⅓ pounds (600g) beets

14 ounces (400g, about 2 medium) potatoes

2 red onions

2 cloves garlic

2 teaspoons whole caraway seeds

2 teaspoons whole fennel seeds

2 tablespoons cooking oil

2 cups (5dl) chicken or vegetable broth

¾ cup (2dl) strong red wine

1 teaspoon granulated sugar

Salt and black pepper

2 apples

5 ounces (150g) goat cheese

1. Peel the beets and potatoes and cut them into ¾-inch (2cm) pieces. Peel and slice the onions and finely chop the garlic. Grind the caraway and fennel seeds in a mortar and pestle.

2. Add the oil to a large pot or pan and sauté the onion, garlic, and the caraway and fennel seeds, until the onions are soft. Add the beets, potatoes, broth, wine, sugar, salt, and pepper, and bring the mixture to a boil.

3. Cook the stew uncovered for 30 minutes, stirring occasionally. Chop the apples finely and stir them into the stew. Let it cook for about 10 more minutes or until the beets are soft. Taste the stew, and then season it with additional salt and pepper, if needed. Crumble the goat cheese and sprinkle it on top of the stew. Serve with an excellent loaf of bread.

ITALIAN CHICKEN STEW

Almost every autumn I spend some time in Italy, harvesting olives from a grove in Umbria until my neck aches, drinking local wine, having pizza for lunch among the gnarled trees, and devoting a coffee break to planning the evening's meal, preferably rabbit stew with white beans and wine. This recipe uses chicken instead of rabbit, but feel free to substitute fresh rabbit if you have access to it.

15 minutes + 40 minutes ■ 4 servings

2 red onions

2 cloves garlic

½ red chile, such as Fresno, seeded

2 medium (200g) carrots

3 celery stalks

1 fennel bulb

1½ oranges (preferably organic)

1 fresh chicken

3 tablespoons olive oil

1¾ cups (4dl) water

1¾ cups (4dl) dry, unoaked white wine

2 14-ounce cans (800g) white beans, drained

Salt and black pepper

TO SERVE

fresh spinach

grated parmesan

bread

1. Peel the onions and cut them into wedges. Peel the garlic and finely chop the garlic and chile. Peel the carrots and cut them and the celery into coarse pieces. Trim the fennel and cut it into small pieces. Wash the oranges and cut them in half. Chop the chicken into 6–8 pieces, and set aside the legs.

2. Add the olive oil to a large pot or saucepan and sauté the onion, garlic, and chile until the onion is soft. Add the carrot, celery, fennel, orange halves, chicken, water, and wine. Bring the mixture to a boil and let it simmer, covered, for about 35 minutes or until all the chicken parts are completely cooked. In the last 10 minutes of cooking time, add the white beans.

3. Remove the chicken and pick the meat from the bones. Remove the orange halves and squeeze any fluid into the stew. Season the stew with salt and pepper and add the chicken back into the mix. Serve the stew with fresh spinach leaves, a generous shaving of Parmesan cheese, and a loaf of good bread on the side.

NOTE If you can find rabbit meat for the stew, cut it into small pieces and fry the meat until golden brown. Place the rabbit meat in the pan with the other ingredients, and add enough water so that the liquid just covers the meat. Cook the stew for about 1½ hours, or until the meat is tender. Expect about 3⅓ pounds (1½ kg) of rabbit meat to make 4 servings.

VENISON GOULASH WITH APPLES AND HORSERADISH

Goulash is a well-loved classic Hungarian dish that only gets better when cooked a few days ahead. Here I have taken a few steps from the traditional recipe and have flirted with other autumn flavors like venison, apple, and root vegetables.

20 minutes + 1½ hours ▪ 4 servings

2 medium (250g) carrots

8 ounces (250g) parsnips

8 ounces (250g, about 2 medium) potatoes

2 red peppers

2 small onions

3 cloves garlic

½ red chile, such as Fresno, seeded

1 pound (500g) venison

3 tablespoons cooking oil

1 tablespoon freshly ground cumin seeds

2 tablespoons smoked paprika

2 tablespoons tomato paste

1–1½ quarts (1–1½ liters) beef broth (not concentrated)

Salt and black pepper

2 apples

FOR SERVING

Greek yoghurt

Fresh horseradish

1 large bunch (250g) of tender parsley, stemmed

1. Peel the carrots, parsnips, and potatoes, and cut them into about ½-inch (1½cm) cubes. Seed the peppers and chop them coarsely. Peel and chop the onion. Peel and finely chop the garlic and finely chop the chili. Trim the meat and cut it into 2-inch (5cm) cubes.

2. Add the cooking oil to a large pot, such as a heavy-bottomed casserole or Dutch oven, and fry the onion, garlic, peppers, chile, and cumin and paprika for a few minutes. Add the meat to the pot and sear everything on high heat until the meat starts to brown on all sides. Lower the heat and add the tomato paste, carrots, parsnips, and potatoes. Pour the broth into the pot, making sure that all the ingredients are covered.

3. Bring the mixture to a boil and let it simmer, covered, for 1–1½ hours or until the meat is tender. During the cooking time, add more liquid to the pot, if needed.

4. Season the mixture with salt and pepper. Peel, core, and finely chop the apples and let them cook in the pot with the other ingredients for the final 5 minutes of cooking time. Fold in most of the chopped parsley, but save some for garnish. Serve the goulash piping hot, together with some horseradish and a dollop of Greek yogurt. Garnish with a scattering of fresh parsley leaves.

BEEF STEW
WITH
FENNEL, PORTER,
AND CHOCOLATE

Malt, water, hops, and yeast. It's crystal clear that beer is just as good in a pot of stew as it is in a glass! With its sweetness and richness, porter is a natural in this context and melds beautifully with fennel, dark chocolate, and the bright citrus notes of freshly squeezed orange.

20 minutes + 1 hour ▪ 4 servings

2 small yellow onions
2 cloves garlic
3 medium (350g) carrots
12 ounces (350g) parsnip
1⅓ pounds (600g) chuck steak
2½ tablespoons whole fennel seeds
3 tablespoons cooking oil
1½–1¾ cups (3½–4dl) porter (dark beer)
1½–1¾ cups (3½–4dl) beef broth
Salt
Freshly ground black pepper
3 ounces (75g) 64–74% dark chocolate
Juice from 1 orange
Cornstarch (optional)

1. Peel and chop the onion and garlic. Peel and cut the carrots and parsnip into small pieces. Trim the meat and cut it into about ½-inch (1½cm) cubes. Grind the fennel seeds.

2. Add the oil to large pot and brown the meat. Stir in the onion, garlic, and ground fennel seeds, and sauté until the onion is soft. Add the carrots, parsnip, porter, and broth. Pour in more broth if the liquid does not cover the meat and vegetables. Season the mixture with salt and pepper, and bring it to a boil.

3. Skim the surface of the broth to remove any excess fat that may have floated to the top, cover the pot, and continue to cook the stew over medium heat for about 1 hour or until the meat is tender. Chop or break the chocolate into small pieces and stir it, together with the orange juice, into the stew. Thicken the stew, if you like, with cornstarch. Serve with boiled or mashed potatoes.

ROOT VEGGIE STEW

Kallops is a classic stew from Sweden that is rich and hearty, made with beef and flavored with bay leaf and allspice. In this version, I've replaced the beef with root vegetables, which work just as well to make a very tasty winter dish. You can replace the veggies with some lightly salted beef brisket, if you're craving a meat stew that comes a little closer to the classic Swedish version of kallops.

10 minutes + 25 minutes ▪ 4 servings

2 yellow onions

1 pound (500g) parsnips

4 large (1 pound; 500g) carrots

1 pound (500g, about 3 large) potatoes

3 tablespoons cooking oil

1 tablespoon ground allspice

4 bay leaves

3⅓ cups (8dl) vegetable broth

Salt and black pepper

Cornstarch (optional)

APPLE SALAD

2 tart apples

¼ cup (½dl) fresh picked thyme leaves

FOR SERVING

crème fraîche or sour cream

1. Peel and coarsely chop the onions. Peel the parsnips, carrots, and potatoes, and cut them into ¾-inch (2cm) pieces. Add the oil to a pot or large saucepan and sauté the onion until it's soft. Add the parsnips, carrots, potatoes, and allspice and crumble the bay leaves into the mixture. Fry briefly. Add the broth, season the mixture with salt and pepper, and bring to a boil.

2. Let the mixture boil, with the cover off, over medium heat for about 25 minutes, or until the vegetables are soft. Season the mixture with salt and pepper and thicken with cornstarch, if you like.

3. To make the apple salad: core the apples and finely slice them (or grate them coarsely). Mix in the thyme leaves. Serve the stew with a dollop of crème fraîche or sour cream and some of the apple salad on top.

HEARTY CHICKEN STEW

This is no ordinary chicken stew—it has a lot going on. Sardines, paprika, olives, and tomatoes add a wonderfully hearty flavor and make this just the right dish for a really gray fall or winter day. If you want a heartier stew or would like to increase the number of servings, just add some more chicken and maybe some big white beans to the mix.

20 minutes + 55 minutes ▪ 4–6 servings

2 red bell peppers

1 orange bell pepper

1 green bell pepper

2 red onions

3 cloves garlic

12 anchovies or sardine fillets in oil

4 ounces (130g, about ¼ cup) pitted black olives, preferably Kalamata

1 large fresh chicken

2 tablespoons olive oil

2½ tablespoons smoked paprika

¾ cup (2dl) water

2 14-ounce cans (800g) diced tomatoes

2 teaspoons salt

1 teaspoon ground black pepper

½ teaspoon sugar

Chopped parsley

1. Core the bell peppers and dice them roughly. Peel and chop the onions and garlic coarsely. Chop the anchovies finely and the olives coarsely. Chop the chicken into 6–8 pieces.

2. Add the olive oil to a large pot or saucepan and brown the chicken pieces. Remove the chicken and then sauté the onion and garlic until soft. Add the peppers, chicken, anchovies, and paprika to the pot and sauté them. Stir in the water, tomatoes, and half the olives. Season the mixture with salt, pepper, and sugar.

3. Bring the mixture to a boil and let it simmer, covered, for 45–50 minutes or until the chicken pieces are cooked through. Remove the chicken pieces from the pan and quickly stir the remaining mixture. Put the chicken pieces back in the pan and sprinkle with the parsley and remaining olives. Serve with rice, orzo, or a loaf of good bread.

PULLED PORK
WITH
BBQ SAUCE

Pulled pork, the classic we love to love! Here, we've put the lid on a wonderful loin of pork with spices, beer, and BBQ sauce, so you can focus on other things while it's in the oven. This is the perfect food to prepare several days in advance, because it only improves with time.

15 minutes + 4 hours in the oven ■ 4 servings

2 teaspoons freshly ground coriander seeds

1 tablespoon strong paprika

1 tablespoon ground cumin

1 tablespoon raw sugar

1 tablespoon salt, plus additional to taste

3½ pounds (1½kg) pork loin

2 large yellow onions

3 cloves garlic

½ red or green chile, seeded (optional)

12 ounces (3½dl) light lager beer

¾ cup (2dl) smoky BBQ sauce, preferably flavored with chipotle (smoked and dried jalapeño)

Juice of 1 lime

Black pepper

1. Preheat the oven to 350°F (175°C). Mix the coriander, paprika, cumin, sugar, and salt in a small bowl. Use a sharp knife to score the meat, and then thoroughly massage it with the spices, making sure to get the spice mix into the cuts as well. Peel and chop the onions. Peel and crush the garlic cloves, and chop the chile if you choose to add it. Then place the onion, garlic, and chile in a large ovenproof casserole (make sure it has a lid that fits securely). Place the meat on top of the onion mixture. Mix the beer and BBQ sauce and pour it over the meat.

2. Cover the casserole with the lid and position it in the center of the oven. Let the meat cook for about 4 hours or until it is so tender that it can easily be pulled apart with a fork. Feel free to baste the meat a few times while it's cooking.

3. Remove the meat from the casserole and whisk the mixture in the pan to make it into a smooth sauce. (Pour a little of the sauce into a bowl and set it aside to serve with the meat.) Pull the meat apart, into thin strands, with a fork and put it back in the pot with the remaining sauce. Mix the meat and sauce with the lime juice, additional salt, and pepper. Serve the pulled pork on soft hamburger buns or French rolls, along with the reserved sauce, and sprinkle some fresh cilantro leaves over the top. Fresh, cool, crunchy coleslaw makes a great side for pulled pork.

> **NOTE** Avoid adding honey to a BBQ sauce that already contains sugar. The two sweeteners fight for attention, and in the end it's just too much of a good thing.

CHUCK STEAK CHILI

This is really my type of stew. You toss delicious things all at once into a big pot, pour in the beer, and put the cover on top. Worry about other things for a few hours and then lift the lid on the ultimate, best-tasting chili. Sheer wizardry. If you want an even heartier chili, you can add cooked beans of your choice at the end.

20 minutes + 2 hours ▪ 6–8 servings

2 yellow onions

3 cloves garlic

1 chipotle (smoked and dried jalapeño)

2 slightly milder dried chiles, such as ancho

2 red bell peppers

4 ounces (140g) bacon

2¼ pounds (1 kg) chuck steak

3 tablespoons cooking oil

2 teaspoons ground cumin

2 teaspoons paprika

1 cinnamon stick

1 cup (2½dl) lager beer

1 14-ounce can (400g) crushed tomatoes

2 cups (5dl) strong beef stock (Note: depending on the size pot you use, you might have to adjust the amount)

Salt and black pepper

1. Peel and chop the onion and garlic. Chop the chipotle and chiles. Seed the bell peppers and cut them into smaller pieces. Thinly slice the bacon. Cut the chuck steak into about ¾-inch (2cm) cubes.

2. Add the oil to a large pot and sear the meat in batches. Remove the meat and set it aside. Sauté the onion, garlic, and chiles until the onion is soft. Add the peppers, bacon, meat, cumin, paprika, and cinnamon stick. Pour in the beer, crushed tomatoes, and stock so that they cover everything and bring the mixture to a boil.

3. Cook the chili, covered, over medium heat for at least 2 hours, or until the meat is very tender. Remove the lid for the second hour to reduce the liquid. Stir occasionally during the cooking time and add more stock if needed. Season the chili with salt and pepper. Serve with tortillas, guacamole, pickled red onions (see recipe below), and lime wedges.

✳ PICKLED RED ONIONS ✳

Peel a red onion and slice it very thinly. In a small bowl, combine the juice of 1 lime and pinch of salt. Add the onion slices to the bowl and use your fingers to thoroughly rub in the mixture. Let it stand for about 20 minutes—and then it's ready! Super tasty for all kinds of tacos, but also with pulled pork.

JULIA CHILD'S COQ AU VIN

Because this is simply the best recipe!

2 hours ■ 4 servings

4 ounces (125g, about 4 slices) thick-cut smoked bacon

7 tablespoons butter, divided

4 pounds (1¾kg) chicken, cut into pieces

Salt and pepper

12–14 small shallots

1 celery stalk, chopped

3 carrots, chopped

3 cloves garlic, minced

⅔ cup (1½dl) brandy

1 bottle of young, full-bodied red wine, such as Beaujolais

1½ tablespoons tomato paste

4–5 thyme sprigs

1 bay leaf

1¼–1¾ cups (3–4dl) chicken stock or strong broth

1¼–1¾ cups (3–4dl) beef stock or broth

8 ounces (225g) small cremini mushrooms

2 tablespoons all-purpose flour

1. Dice the bacon. Add 3 tablespoons of the butter to a large pot—a Dutch oven or a heavy-bottomed casserole would be ideal—and fry the bacon in the butter. Remove the bacon and set it aside. Brown the chicken in the same pot and season it with a little salt and pepper. Remove the chicken pieces from the pot and set them aside. Add the shallots, celery, carrots, and garlic to the pot and brown them in the butter and bacon fat. Add the fried bacon and chicken to the pot. Put the lid on the pot and cook the mixture over low heat for about 10 minutes. Making sure the stove fan is off, remove the lid and add the brandy. Shake the pot and ignite the brandy with a lighted match. Continue to shake the pot back and forth for several seconds until the flames have been extinguished. Pour in the wine and stir in the tomato paste, thyme, and bay leaf. Season with salt and pepper. Add the chicken and beef stocks (or broths) to cover. Let the mixture simmer, covered, for about 1½ hours, or until the meat is completely tender.

2. In the meantime, place the mushrooms, whole or quartered, depending on size, in a dry pan and cook them over medium-high heat until they begin sizzling and snapping. Add 2 tablespoons of butter and sauté until golden brown.

3. Remove the chicken pieces from the pot and set them aside. Simmer the mixture in the pot, uncovered, until about 2 cups (5dl) of liquid remains. In a small bowl, blend the remaining 2 tablespoons of butter and the flour into a thick paste, and then whisk it into the hot liquid in the pot, stirring it for a few minutes. The sauce should be thick enough to lightly coat the back of a spoon. Transfer the chicken and mushrooms to the pot and baste with the sauce. Serve with green beans and mashed potatoes.

QUICK AND EASY SKILLET MEALS

LL-IN-ONE DISHES ARE TRUE LIFESAVERS. They're full of flavor and light on cleanup, and what's not to love about that? They're also quick: most of the recipes in this chapter, which can be prepared in a skillet, don't take more than 45 minutes, and they're easy to make, too.

And, to make wintertime fare a little more exciting, I've included an assortment of recipes with delicious flavors from sunny climates around the world—from huevos rancheros, moussaka, and saltimbocca to more familiar favorites like omelets and good old hamburgers and hot dogs.

VEAL MEATBALLS
IN
DILL SAUCE

I really like veal in dill sauce, but it takes a while to make it the classic way, so I was excited when I first thought about veal *meatballs* in dill sauce. Fantastic! Here, I use real cream and organic veal.

40–45 minutes ▪ 4 servings

MEATBALLS

½ onion

2 tablespoons butter

2 tablespoons bread crumbs

1½ tablespoons concentrated beef stock

3 tablespoons heavy cream

18 ounces (500g) ground veal

1 tablespoon cider vinegar

1 teaspoon sugar

Salt and white pepper

SAUCE

1½ onion

3 medium (300g) carrots

1¼ cups (6dl) cooking water from meatballs

1 cup (2½dl) heavy cream

2½ tablespoons cider vinegar

½ tablespoons granulated sugar

2 tablespoons (35g) fresh dill, finely chopped

Salt and white pepper

About 2 tablespoons cornstarch

1. To make the meatballs: Peel and finely chop the onion and fry in the butter until soft. Mix the bread crumbs, concentrated beef stock, and cream in a large bowl and let it stand for a few minutes. Add the cooked onion, meat, vinegar, and sugar to the bowl and quickly work everything together into a smooth and pliable mixture. Season with salt and pepper.

2. Fill a pot with salted water and bring it to a boil. Shape the mixture into small meatballs (try not to overwork it, or the meatballs will be dense and tough) and boil them 2–3 at a time (depending on the pot size) for 4–5 minutes or until the meatballs are completely cooked through. Remove the meatballs with a slotted spoon (save the cooking water) and put them aside while you make the sauce.

3. To make the sauce: Peel and cut the onion for the sauce in the rough wedges. Peel and cut the carrots into rough coins. Mix the cooking water, cream, vinegar, sugar, and dill in a large pot and bring to a boil. Season with salt and pepper. Add the onion and carrots and cook, covered, on low heat until the carrots are soft. Mix about ½ cup (1 dl) of the cooking water with the cornstarch. Pour this into the sauce again and let everything come to a boil. Add the meatballs to the sauce, and let them warm up. Season with salt and pepper and serve with boiled potatoes, if you like.

SARDINE AND SAGE FRITTATA

The frittata is one of my favorite versions of the classic omelet, my savior when it comes to quick lunches and cleaning out the refrigerator. I usually have some potatoes around to make this omelet more filling, but you can add just about anything to it and it taste delicious. The sky's the limit!

30 minutes ▪ 4 servings

4 large potatoes

2 small onions

2 cloves garlic

4 sardines

10–12 sage leaves

3 tablespoons olive oil

8 eggs

½ cup (1 dl) milk

Salt and black pepper

¾ cup (2dl) finely grated Parmesan or Pecorino cheese

1. Preheat the oven to 350°F (175°C). Peel the potatoes and slice them as thinly as possible. Peel and slice the onions and garlic. Chop the sardines and sage leaves coarsely.

2. Add the olive oil to a large ovenproof skillet and fry the potatoes over medium heat, gently stirring now and then, until they're almost soft. Add the onion, garlic, and sage and cook until the onion is soft.

3. In a large bowl, whisk together the eggs and milk. Season with salt and pepper. Pour the egg mixture into the pan. Sprinkle in the chopped sardines and cook the egg mixture over low heat, without stirring it, until the mixture has set, about 8–12 minutes.

4. Distribute the grated cheese over the eggs and place the pan in the oven. Bake the frittata for about 10 minutes, or until the surface is golden brown. Serve it immediately with a crisp, green salad.

RICOTTA AND PESTO OMELET

I tend to fixate on certain flavors and dishes from time to time. I enjoyed this take on the classic omelet, for example, with its delicious mix of pesto and ricotta, for breakfast on countless mornings in Cape Town during a vacation a number of years ago. And it is still a favorite! The secret to this delightfully creamy omelet is not to cook it too long. It's also important to use a really good pesto. You can buy perfectly good pesto in the supermarket these days, but it is so easy to make and tastes so much fresher and brighter if you make it yourself.

20 minutes ▪ 4 servings

8 eggs

½ cup (1 dl) milk or water

Salt

2 tablespoons butter or canola oil

¾ cup (2dl) ricotta

⅔ cup (1½dl) good pesto

4 slices of toast (optional)

Flaked salt and freshly ground pepper

NOTE To make your own pesto, add a couple of cups of fresh basil, a clove garlic, a small handful of toasted pine nuts or walnuts, a pinch of salt, about ½ cup grated Parmesan cheese, juice from half a lemon and ¾ cups of olive oil to a food processor and pulse to the desired consistency.

1. In a large bowl, gently whisk together the eggs, milk, and salt. Add the butter to the skillet and pour in the egg mixture. Cook over low heat without stirring the egg mixture until it has set but is still a little creamy.

2. With a spatula, gently loosen the omelet around the edges of the pan and spread the ricotta and pesto over half the omelet (the half closest to the handle). Tilt the pan away from you. Run the spatula around the empty half of the omelet, gently lift it up, and fold it over. Slide the omelet out of the pan and onto a plate. Sprinkle a little flaked salt and coarsely ground pepper over the top and serve immediately. If you like, serve the omelet with warm buttered toast (a light sourdough is a great option).

MUSHROOM HASH
WITH
BRUSSELS SPROUTS
AND APPLES

Mushrooms, Brussels sprouts, and apples. All good things come in threes, and that's definitely true in this amazingly good cold-weather hash. If you want to make it more luxurious, you can add some cream at the end and let it warm through for a few minutes.

About 20 minutes ▪ 4 servings

1 large yellow onion

7 ounces (200g) fresh brussels sprouts

7 ounces (200g) chanterelles, or other forest mushrooms such as porcini, portabella, or shiitake

2 tart apples

1¾ pounds (800g, about 4 large) potatoes

2 tablespoons butter

1 teaspoon freshly ground caraway seeds

Salt and black pepper

Grated Parmesan or Pecorino cheese

1. Peel and slice the onion and cut the Brussels sprouts into quarters. Clean the mushrooms and cut them into small pieces if they are large. Core the apples and cut them into small cubes. Set aside while preparing the potatoes.

2. Peel the potatoes and cut them into ⅓-inch (1 cm) cubes. Add the butter to a large skillet and fry the potatoes and caraway seeds over medium heat until the potatoes are almost soft. Stir the mixture occasionally while it's cooking to keep the potatoes from sticking to the bottom of the pan and burning. They're done when they've turned golden brown.

3. Add the onion, Brussels sprouts, and mushrooms to the pan and fry the mixture until the mushrooms begin to brown. Lower the heat and cover the pan with a lid or aluminum foil and continue to cook until the Brussels sprouts are almost soft. This takes a couple of minutes. Add the apples and cook for another couple of minutes, stirring the mixture while it cooks. Season with salt and pepper and serve with grated Parmesan cheese.

CHEESE-FILLED HAMBURGERS WITH CARAMELIZED ONIONS

Sometimes you just need to get some hot food on the table quickly. If your kids love burgers—and you love steak and onions—this recipe will satisfy everyone's cravings and beat the clock at the same time. If you don't have any chèvre on hand, use cream cheese or mascarpone. They won't have the same tang as goat cheese, but they'll provide an equally pleasant creaminess. Give it a try!

About 30 minutes ▪ 4 servings

2 cloves garlic

1⅓ pounds (600g) ground beef

1 egg

2 tablespoons heavy cream

2 tablespoons concentrated beef broth

1 teaspoon salt

Freshly ground black pepper

3 ounces (100g) chèvre

¼ cup (30g) pine nuts

CARAMELIZED ONIONS

4 onions

3 tablespoons butter

1 pinch of sugar

1 pinch of salt

1. Grate the garlic and place it in a large bowl with the ground beef, egg, cream, beef broth, and salt and pepper. Using your hands or a fork, gently and quickly mix the ingredients (don't overwork the meat, otherwise it will get tough). Break the chèvre into small pieces. Toast the pine nuts quickly in a dry skillet until they are golden brown.
2. Gently shape the meat mixture into four balls, and use your thumb to make a deep indentation in each ball. Press the cheese and toasted pine nuts into the middle of each ball and cover it completely with the meat. Flatten the balls slightly with your palm to about ¾-inch (2cm) thick and set them aside.
3. Slice the onions. Add the butter to a frying pan and sauté the onions over medium heat. While the onions are cooking, add the sugar and salt, and continue to cook the onions until they've become soft and start to get some color. Check them every 5–10 minutes to make sure they don't burn. Stir the onions and continue to cook them for another 10 minutes or so. After 20 minutes, the onions should be very soft and just caramelized, with brown spots here and there. Set the onions aside and keep them warm.
4. Fry the burgers in the same frying pan (add more butter to the pan, if needed) over medium heat until they are nicely browned and cooked through. Place the burgers in a dish and cover them with foil to keep them warm. Stir about ⅔ cup (1½dl) of water into the pan, reduce to about half and pour the light gravy over the burgers. Top them with the caramelized onions and serve immediately with boiled potatoes or roasted root vegetables.

JANSSON'S HASH

In Sweden we cook potatoes with lots of cream, onion, and a salty pickled fish in a gratin and serve it at Christmas dinner. It might sound a bit strange, but we call it Jansson's Temptation, and it is just tempting! I've started to make this as a quick hash instead, and it´s so delicious. In this version, I've added some peas and dill and some nice anchovies. The original fish; *anjovis*, you have to come to Sweden to enjoy!

About 20 minutes ■ **4 servings**

1¾ pounds (800g, about 4 large) potatoes

3 tablespoons butter

½ leek

1 small onion

2 cups (5dl) frozen peas, thawed

½ cup (1 dl) chopped dill

Salt and white pepper

5–8 anchovy fillets (depending on size)

¾ cup (2dl) heavy cream

4 egg yolks (for eating raw)

1. Peel the potatoes and cut into ⅓-inch (1 cm) cubes. Add the butter to a large frying pan and fry the potatoes over medium heat until they're almost soft. While the potatoes are cooking, stir them from time to time, to make sure they don't burn. You want them to turn golden brown.

2. In the meantime, slice the leek and rinse it carefully to get rid of any sand or grit. Peel the onion and chop it. When the potatoes are soft, add the leeks and onions to the pan.

3. Fry the mixture on low heat until the onion has softened. Add the peas and dill, and season it with the salt, pepper, and finely chopped anchovies. Continue to fry the mixture until the peas are warm. Add the cream and cook for a minute while continuously stirring the mixture. Place the raw egg yolks on top. Serve with a crusty loaf of bread, a bottle of good beer, and a shot of schnapps on the side.

NOTE Eating raw or undercooked eggs can pose a health risk, especially to the elderly, young children under the age of four, pregnant women, and other highly susceptible individuals with compromised immune systems. Make sure that foods that contain raw or lightly cooked eggs are made only with pasteurized eggs. Cooking eggs reduces the risk of illness.

MOUSSAKA

Moussaka holds a place in my kitchen a bit like a forgotten vacation from the past. But sometimes the memories swirl up and I get an insane craving for this rich gratin. Here, I keep it easy by making everything in the same pan. No hassle, but lots of flavor! I prefer zucchini, instead of eggplant, in this dish. Don't forget to add the lemon zest. It brings a bright zing to this moussaka and stirs up memories of Mediterranean sunshine and warm days, even in the depth of winter.

About 1 hour ▪ 4 servings

1 large yellow onion

2 cloves garlic

1 red chile, such as Fresno, seeded

3 tablespoons olive oil

1 pound (500g) ground lamb or beef

1 14-ounce can (400g) crushed tomatoes

1 tablespoon dried mint

2 bay leaves, crumbled

1¼ cups (3dl) water

Salt and black pepper

4 ounces (130g, about ¼ cup) pitted black Kalamata olives

1 large zucchini

8 ounces (250g) fresh mozzarella

Grated zest of 1 large lemon (preferably organic)

1. Preheat the oven to 350°F (175°C). Peel and finely chop the onion and garlic. Finely chop the chile.

2. Add the olive oil to a wide, ovenproof skillet or cast iron frying pan. Brown the meat, then add the onion, garlic, and chile, and fry until the onion is soft. Add crushed tomatoes, mint, and bay leaves. Add the water to the pan. Season the mixture with salt and pepper, and bring it to a boil.

3. Reduce the heat to medium, and cook the mixture, uncovered, for 25–30 minutes. Stir it occasionally while it's cooking.

4. Stir the olives into the meat sauce. Cut the zucchini into ¼-inch (1 cm) slices and press them gently into the meat sauce. Tear the mozzarella into small pieces and sprinkle them over the top. Finish the dish with the lemon zest.

5. Bake the moussaka on the middle rack of the oven for about 25 minutes, or until the zucchini is soft and the mozzarella is golden brown and bubbling in places. Let the moussaka rest for about 15 minutes before serving.

HUEVOS RANCHEROS

This is the egg dish of all egg dishes, with a tortilla bottom, fried beans and sunny-side-up eggs on top, finished with homemade salsa, cilantro, and cheese. Do I even need to say this is good? It is S-U-P-E-R-G-O-O-D.

30 minutes ■ 4 servings

SALSA

1 small onion

1 clove garlic

2 large tomatoes

1 jalapeño, seeded and minced

½ teaspoon salt

½ teaspoon sugar

Black pepper

1 teaspoon ground cumin

Juice of ½ lime

FRIED BEANS

1 large yellow onion

2 cloves garlic

2 tablespoons cooking oil

2 14-ounce cans (800g) black beans, drained

½ cup of water

Salt and black pepper

4 eggs

FOR THE TOPPING AND ASSEMBLY

4 corn tortillas

4 ounces (125g) fresh mozzarella

5 ounces (140g) feta cheese, crumbled

Handful of fresh cilantro, coarsely chopped

1. For the salsa, peel and roughly chop the onion and garlic. Coarsely chop the tomatoes and then mix the chopped ingredients with the jalapeño. Place everything in a small saucepan and add the salt, sugar, pepper, cumin, and lime juice. Bring the mixture to a boil and let it simmer over medium heat for about 10 minutes, until the salsa comes together. Add a little water, if the salsa starts to get dry (some tomatoes are juicier than others).

2. Wrap the tortillas in foil and place them in a 375°F (190°C) oven for 10–15 minutes to warm.

3. For the fried beans, peel and thinly slice the onion. Peel and finely chop the garlic. Put the oil in a saucepan or skillet and sauté the onion and garlic until the onion is soft. Add the beans, mashing them into the onion and garlic mixture, add the water and continue to fry it for a couple of minutes until the water has cooked into the beans. While the beans are cooking, give them a stir from time to time. Season with salt and pepper.

4. Make four wells in the bean mixture and crack an egg into each one of them. Fry the eggs until the whites have cooked but the yolks are still creamy. Spice with salt and pepper.

5. Tear the mozzarella into pieces and mix it with the feta cheese. Put a warm tortilla on each plate. Spoon the bean mixture and eggs on top of the tortillas, and top them off with the salsa and cheese blend. Garnish with a sprinkling of fresh cilantro and serve immediately.

PORK CHOPS SALTIMBOCCA

Saltimbocca is traditionally made with veal, but it's just as delicious, and much more wallet-friendly, when it's prepared with pork. Ask your butcher to cut the prosciutto into 1/16-inch (1 mm) slices.

About 40 minutes ■ **4 servings**

3 medium (300g) carrots

4 celery stalks

2 small onions

3 cloves garlic

½ red chile, such as Fresno, seeded

4 bone-in pork chops

Salt and pepper

12 large sage leaves

8 slices prosciutto

2 tablespoons olive oil

2 14-ounce cans (800g) crushed tomatoes

1¼ cups (3dl) dry, unoaked white wine

½ teaspoon sugar (optional)

1. Peel and dice the carrots finely. Slice the celery. Peel and finely chop the onions and garlic. Finely chop the chile. Season the chops with salt and pepper. Top each of the chops with 3 sage leaves and then wrap 2 slices of prosciutto around each chop.

2. Add the olive oil to a wide saucepan or frying pan, with high edges, and brown the chops on both sides. Remove the chops and put them aside. Fry the onion, garlic, and chile in the same pan until the onions are soft. Add the carrots and celery and fry them for a few more minutes. Stir in the crushed tomatoes and wine and cook the mixture, uncovered, for about 15 minutes or so. Season the mixture with salt and pepper. Add the sugar, if you like.

3. Put the chops back in the pan with the other ingredients, and let the mixture simmer, covered, for about 15 minutes. Baste the chops with the liquid in the pan, a few times, while the mixture is cooking. Serve the saltimbocca with a loaf of good bread.

In Italian, *salti* and *bocca* mean "jump" and "mouth." Saltimbocca certainly describes the pork dish above: it's so incredibly good it just jumps into your mouth!

HOT DOGS
WITH
BALSAMIC BRAISED CABBAGE

Have I said that I like hot dogs? No, I take that back. I *love* hot dogs! Good hot dogs, along with all the fixings, are the answer to world peace and the meaning of life, if you ask me. Balsamic braised cabbage is the perfect accompaniment to good quality hot dogs. Add some strong Dijon mustard to the mix and you have a meal that certainly does not have to apologize for itself.

30 minutes ▪ 4 servings

2 yellow onions

14 ounces (400g, about ½ head) white cabbage

3 tablespoons butter

1¼ cups (3dl) red wine

¾ cup (2dl) balsamic vinegar

5 tablespoons sugar

3 bay leaves

Salt and black pepper

½ stalk celery

1 bay leaf

1 teaspoon peppercorns

4 hot dogs or as many as you wish to serve

4 hot dog buns or as many as you wish to serve

Dijon mustard

1. Peel and slice the onions and finely shred the cabbage. Add the butter to large pot or a pan and sauté the onions until soft. Add the cabbage, wine, vinegar, sugar, and bay leaves.

2. Season the mixture with salt and pepper and let it simmer, covered, over low heat, for about 25 minutes or until the cabbage is completely soft. Stir the mixture occasionally, while it simmers.

3. Meanwhile, prepare the hot dogs. Chop the celery. Fill a saucepan halfway with water and add the celery, bay leaf, peppercorns, and hot dogs. Bring to a boil. Take out the hot dogs when they are warm; if you leave them too long, there's a risk that they might crack – but if that happens, don't worry—they will be just as tasty!

4. Top each hot dog, in its bun, with a serving of the braised cabbage—and don't forget to use some Dijon mustard!

BUTTER-FRIED COD
WITH
SHRIMP AND DILL

Contrary to what you might think, fish is not difficult to cook. In fact, it's a breeze, if you use good ingredients and follow this insanely simple recipe. The only equipment you need is a frying pan, and cleanup takes no time at all. I like to serve this dish with a loaf of really good bread, for dipping in the pan, of course (it's that good), but some parsley-tossed, oven-roasted root vegetables make a delicious side dish as well.

20 minutes ▪ 4 servings

4 hard-boiled eggs

½ cup (1 dl) small capers

4 whole pickled beets

14 ounces (400g) cooked shrimp (I prefer the ones you peel yourself)

1 pound (500g) fresh boneless, skinless cod fillet

Salt and black pepper

3 tablespoons butter

½ cup (1 dl) chopped dill

1. Finely chop the eggs, capers, and beets. Peel the shrimp if you bought the ones with shell still on. Set all to the side.

2. Dry the cod fillet with paper towels and season it with salt and pepper. Add the butter to medium-size frying pan and wait until the butter has melted and stopped sizzling. Add the cod to the pan and fry it over high heat, basting it with the butter, for 2–3 minutes. Lower the heat, and fry the fish on the other side, for about 3 minutes and continue to baste it with the butter.

3. Top the fish with the shrimp, egg, capers, beets and dill and serve immediately.

To keep your cast iron cookware clean—and to prolong its life—never use detergent! Wash your cast iron pot or pan with hot water when it's still hot, so it's easier to clean, and dry it immediately to reduce the risk of rust. For more information about how to care for your cast iron cookware, take a look at page ix, and discover how a little tender loving care can extend the use of your equipment and also give you better results when you use it.

MEATBALLS
WITH
TOMATO SAUCE
AND WHITE BEANS

When you cook meatballs in tomato sauce, they taste fantastic. This recipe is rustic, simple, and delicious!

about 35 minutes ▪ 4 servings

FOR THE SAUCE

2 stalks celery

2 carrots (200g)

½ yellow onion

2–3 cloves garlic

½ red chile, such as Fresno, seeded

2 tablespoons olive oil

2 14-ounce cans (800g) crushed tomatoes

1 teaspoon sugar

Salt and black pepper

FOR THE MEATBALLS

½ onion

1 clove garlic

1 tablespoon olive oil

1 pound (500g) ground meat

Fine sea salt

Freshly ground black pepper

1 14-ounce can (400g) cooked white beans

½–⅔ cups (1–1½dl) shredded basil

Grated Parmesan cheese

1. To make the sauce: Slice the celery. Finely chop the carrots, onions, garlic, and chile. Add the olive oil to a large frying pan or saucepan and sauté the onion, garlic, and chile until the onion is soft. Add the celery and carrots and continue to sauté for a few minutes. Stir the crushed tomatoes and sugar into the mixture and bring it to a boil. Let the mixture simmer, covered, for about 10 minutes, stirring occasionally. Season with salt and pepper.
2. To make the meatballs: Finely chop the onion and the garlic. Add the olive oil to a small pan and sauté the chopped onion and garlic on low heat until soft. Let the onion cool slightly and then combine in a bowl with the ground meat, salt, and pepper, into a smooth mixture. Shape the mixture into large meatballs, about 1¼ inches (3cm) wide.
3. Put the meatballs into the pan and cover them completely with the tomato sauce. Cook the meatballs, covered, over medium heat for about 10 minutes, or until the meatballs are completely cooked. Add the white beans to the pan and let them warm through in the last 3–4 minutes of cooking time. Add the shredded basil and some Parmesan cheese to the pan. Serve with a loaf of good bread.

THE WORLD'S BEST FRIED CHICKEN

Sometimes you want a taste of sunny, summertime picnic food in the dead of winter and crave something crunchy, savory, and easy to eat. This recipe for insanely good fried chicken fits the bill. The secret is to marinate the chicken in buttermilk overnight, or even for a just few hours. Combine some hoisin sauce with an equal amount of sweet chili sauce, and you have the perfect dip for this fried chicken.

30 minutes + 3 hours in the refrigerator ▪ 4 servings

FOR THE CHICKEN

2 pounds (1 kg) chicken legs with skin

2 cups (4dl) buttermilk, divided

1–2 quarts (1–2 liters, depending on pan size) cooking oil

2 cups (4dl) rice flour

1 tablespoon sea salt

1 tablespoon coarsely ground black pepper

1 tablespoon onion powder

1 tablespoon ground coriander

1 tablespoon ground cumin

1 egg white

FOR SERVING

½ cup (1 dl) hoisin sauce

½ cup (1 dl) sweet chili sauce

FOR GARNISH

1 handful cilantro, chopped (optional)

1. Put the chicken legs in a large freezer bag and cover them with 1 cup of the buttermilk. Seal the bag securely, and let the chicken marinate in the refrigerator for at least 3 hours or, preferably, overnight. (You can also start marinating the chicken in the morning and prepare it in the evening.) Remove the legs from the marinade in the freezer bag and let them drain slightly. Set them aside.

2. Fill a large pot with salted water and bring it to a boil. Reduce the heat to medium-low and add the chicken legs to the pot. Cook them for 15–20 minutes, until they are fully cooked. (At this point, if you plan to prepare the chicken at a later date, you can refrigerate the chicken legs. Just be sure to let the warm up gently before you prep and fry them.)

3. Mix the hoisin sauce and sweet chili sauce and let stand until ready to serve.

4. Heat the frying oil in a large, deep frying pan with high sides or a large, deep pot until the oil reaches a temperature of 350°F (180°C). (If your stove fan is on, turn it off. Make sure you have the lid handy just in case the oil catches fire. If it does, immediately cover the pan and turn off the heat.)

5. Mix the rice flour, sea salt, pepper, onion powder, coriander, and cumin. Whisk the egg white until it is foamy and mix it with the remaining 1 cup of buttermilk. Dip each chicken leg in the egg mixture and then roll it in the seasoned flour, making sure that each drumstick is completely coated.

6. Fry the drumsticks in the oil, 4–5 at a time, until they are golden brown. Remove the chicken and drain it on paper towels. Fry the rest of the chicken and serve it immediately with the hoisin–sweet chili sauce blend. Sprinkle some freshly chopped cilantro on top of the sauce, if you like. Enjoy!

HEARTY WINTER CASSEROLES

Cod, Shrimp, and Fennel Casserole, 60

Couscous-Stuffed Roast Chicken, 63

Potato Gratin Deluxe, 64

Roast Pork Belly with Fennel and Lemon, 67

Baked Curry Chicken with Butternut Squash
and Root Vegetables, 68

Cabbage and Lamb Casserole, 71

Mackerel and Chanterelle Gratin, 72

Bacon and Roasted Root Vegetable "Pancake," 75

Shepherd's Pie with Smoked Pork Sausage, 76

Oven-Roasted Italian Sausage with Tomatoes
and Fennel, 79

Veggie and Gorgonzola Stew, 80

hen it's cold outside and the snow is flying, there's nothing better than a decadent, comforting meal that you can bring to the table and serve straight from the pan. I love how simple it is to fill a casserole with tasty things, tuck it into the oven, and let it turn into the ultimate delicious meal. You'll find plenty of these in this chapter, from a deluxe potato gratin and a roasted couscous-stuffed chicken to an addictive pork belly dish. You'll also discover an energizing veggie stew with Gorgonzola and a savory cabbage pudding. There are a couple unusual and delicious fish recipes here, too. Even if you're not convinced you'll like it, try the Mackerel (yes, mackerel) and Chanterelle Gratin and become a convert!

COD, SHRIMP, AND FENNEL CASSEROLE

I know, I know, a fish casserole doesn't sound very sexy, but this one is. I've used a cod fillet here, but another firm, white fish would be just as excellent. Either way, this dish will make you feel all warm and fuzzy inside. Comfort food at its best!

1 hour ■ 4 servings

1 large yellow onion
1 tablespoon butter
1¾ pounds (800g) boiled and peeled potatoes
1 small bulb of fennel
14 ounces (400g) cod fillet
4 ounces (100g) peeled shrimp
½ cup (1 dl) finely chopped dill, packed
Zest of 1 lemon (preferably organic)
4 eggs
1¼ cups (3dl) heavy cream
¼ cup (½dl) unoaked, dry white wine
Salt and pepper

1. Preheat the oven to 450°F (225°C). Peel and slice the onion. Add the butter to a skillet and sauté the onion until it's soft. Cut the potatoes into thick slices. Clean and thinly slice the fennel. Cut the cod into 2¾-inch (7cm pieces). Layer the potatoes, onions, fennel, fish, shrimp, dill and lemon zest in a greased casserole.

2. In a bowl, stir together the eggs, cream, and wine. Season the mixture with salt and pepper and pour it into the casserole. Give the casserole a gentle shake to help distribute the liquid evenly. Bake on the middle rack of the oven for about 40 minutes or until it turns golden brown.

COUSCOUS-STUFFED ROAST CHICKEN

I once found myself in conversation with a man from the Middle East, and when I asked him what he missed the most from his homeland, he gave me his favorite recipe for couscous-filled lamb. I decided to try something similar with chicken, and it's so good

20 minutes + 1 ½ hours ■ 4 servings

COUSCOUS FILLING

3 ounces (100g, about 10 whole) dried apricots

¾ cup (2dl) couscous

2 tablespoons melted butter

1 teaspoon strong paprika

1 teaspoon ground cumin

1 teaspoon salt

½ cup (1 dl) raisins

2 cups (4½dl) hot water

CHICKEN

2 cloves garlic

2 lemons (preferably organic)

3 tablespoons softened butter

1 teaspoon cinnamon

1 teaspoon strong paprika

1 teaspoon ground cumin

1 tablespoon honey

2 teaspoons salt

½ teaspoon ground black pepper

1 fresh chicken

5 large (1⅓ pounds; 600g) carrots

2 yellow onions

1. Preheat the oven to 450°F (225°C).

2. To make the filling: Roughly chop the apricots and mix them with the couscous, butter, paprika, cumin, salt, and raisins in a saucepan or bowl with a lid. Add the hot water and stir the mixture. Let it rest, covered, while you prepare the chicken.

3. For the chicken: Peel and grate the garlic. Juice 1 of the lemons. In a small bowl, combine the garlic with the lemon juice, butter, cinnamon, paprika, cumin, honey, salt, and pepper to form a paste. Rub the chicken with the mixture, including under the skin. Set aside.

4. Peel the carrots and onions and wash the remaining lemon. Cut the onion and lemon into wedges and the carrots in large pieces. Place the lemon and the vegetables in a large ovenproof casserole or pot.

5. Stuff the chicken with as much of the couscous mixture as will fit and spread the rest over the vegetables in the casserole. Place the chicken on top, cover the casserole with the lid (or aluminum foil), and put it in the oven.

6. Roast for about 1–1½ hours, (uncovered for the last 30 minutes) or until the chicken is cooked through and the skin is golden brown. To test for doneness, make a small cut in the skin between the leg and the breast. If the juice runs clear, the chicken is done. If the juice is slightly pink, keep the chicken in the oven and check again in a few minutes. When the chicken is done, let it rest for about 10–15 minutes before carving it. Serve the chicken with the roasted veggie-couscous mixture.

POTATO GRATIN DELUXE

Creamy potato gratin is always a favorite, and here I make it a little extra exciting with wax beans, mushrooms, and prosciutto. This dish is hearty enough to be served all on its own, but of course it is also a supergood accompaniment to a fine piece of meat.

About 55 minutes ▪ 4–5 Servings

2¼ pounds (1 kg) russet potatoes

1 large yellow onion

10 ounces (300g) chanterelle or cremini mushrooms

7 ounces (200g) wax beans, green beans, or haricots verts

10–12 slices prosciutto

2 tablespoons butter

1½ ounces (50g, about ½ cup) finely grated Parmesan cheese

Salt and black pepper

1¼ cups (5dl) heavy cream

½ cup (2dl) milk

1. Preheat the oven to 400°F (200°C). Peel and thinly slice the potatoes and the onion. Clean the mushrooms, and if you like, cut them into small pieces. Trim the beans and slice them straight down the middle. Cut the slices of prosciutto in half.

2. Add the butter to a frying pan and sauté the mushrooms and onion. Layer the sliced potatoes, beans, mushrooms, prosciutto, and grated cheese in a casserole or deep baking dish with high sides, seasoning with salt and pepper between the layers, and finishing with a layer of potatoes. Mix the cream and milk in a bowl and pour the mixture over the potatoes.

3. Place the baking dish on a rack in the lower half of the oven and bake for 35–45 minutes or until the potatoes feel soft and the gratin is golden brown.

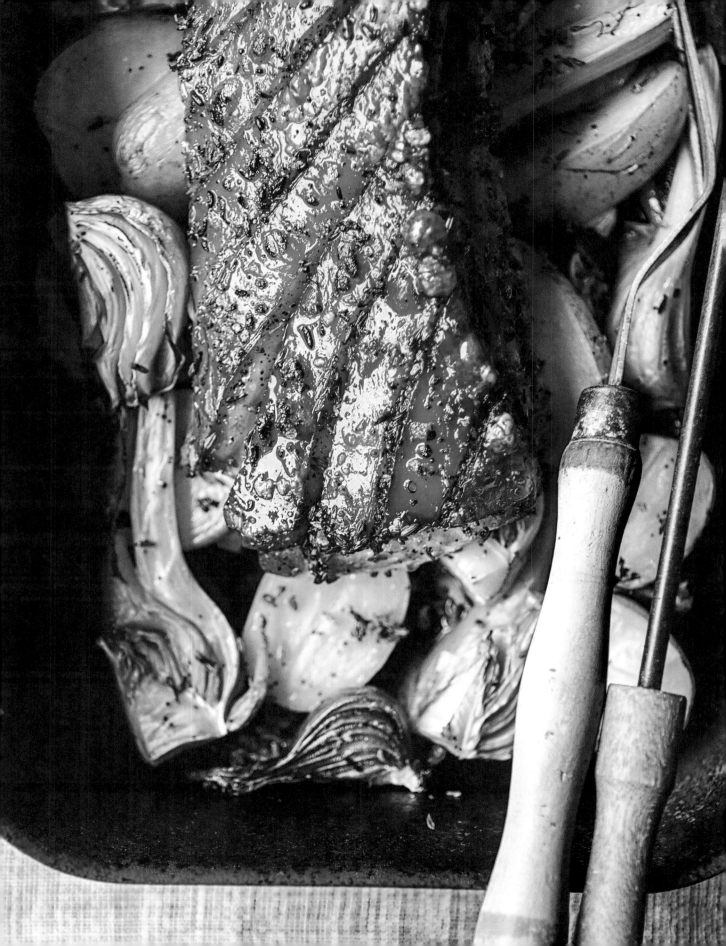

ROAST PORK BELLY
WITH
FENNEL AND LEMON

Mama mia! Fennel seeds, lemon, and garlic together with lightly salted pork are so good they can almost turn vegetarians into carnivores. If you're ever tempted to grill in autumn—or even in the depths of winter—I can promise that the result gets even better if you finish the pork on the grill, over high heat.

10 minutes + about 1 ½ hours ▪ 4–6 servings

4–5 cloves garlic, divided

2 tablespoons whole fennel seeds

Grated zest of 1½ lemons (preferably organic)

Salt

1 teaspoon freshly ground black pepper

1¾ pounds (800g) salted pork belly with the fat

1¾ pounds (800g) potatoes

2 red onions

2 average-size fennel bulbs

1. Preheat the oven to 350°F (175°C). Peel 2 of the garlic cloves and mash them into the fennel seeds, lemon zest, salt, and black pepper to make a rub. With a sharp knife, make slits in the fat layer of the pork belly and thoroughly massage the rub into the meat.

2. Peel the potatoes and onions and cut them into thin wedges. Trim the fennel bulbs and also cut them into thin wedges. Peel and crush the remaining 2–3 cloves garlic. Transfer all to a large casserole or baking dish and season the veggies with a little salt. Place the pork on top with the fat layer facing up.

3. Put the baking dish on a rack in the middle of the oven and roast the pork until the internal temperature is 140°F (60°C). Use a kitchen thermometer for the best results. Raise the heat to 485°F (250°C) and continue to roast the meat until the internal temperature is 160–165°F (70–74°C) and the skin is puffy and crispy.

4. Cut the meat into thin slices and serve it immediately with the vegetables from the pan and, if you like, a creamy coleslaw.

BAKED CURRY CHICKEN WITH BUTTERNUT SQUASH AND ROOT VEGETABLES

This is serious comfort food, and the combination of spices gives this dish both warmth and a nice kick. The secret to a really juicy chicken is to do your utmost to get the butter under the skin.

20 minutes + about 1 ½ hours ▪ 4 servings

VEGETABLE BLEND

1⅓ pounds (600g, 1 small) butternut squash

1¾ pounds (800g) potatoes

3 medium (300g) carrots

2 large red onions

2 cloves garlic

½–1 red chile, such as Fresno, seeded

2-inch piece (25g) fresh ginger

1 large lemon (preferably organic)

2 tablespoons olive oil

Salt

CHICKEN

1–2 cloves garlic

3 tablespoons softened butter

1½ tablespoons curry powder

2 teaspoons ground cumin

2 teaspoons salt

Black pepper

1 tablespoon honey

1 fresh chicken

1. Preheat the oven to 350°F (175°C).

2. For the vegetable blend: Peel the squash, potatoes, carrots, and onions and cut everything into 1-inch pieces. Peel and chop the garlic and the chile. Peel the ginger (see prep tip, below) and chop it finely. Cut the lemon into wedges. Mix everything in a roasting pan along with the olive oil. Season with salt.

3. For the chicken: Peel and finely chop the garlic and mash it into the butter, curry powder, cumin, salt, black pepper, and honey to make a pasty spice rub. Thoroughly massage the chicken with the rub and get as much of it as possible under the skin.

4. Place the chicken on top of the vegetables in the roasting pan. Place the pan on the bottom rack of the oven and bake the chicken until it is cooked through, about 1 hour and 20 minutes. Baste the chicken with the melted butter every 15–20 minutes or so during the cooking time.

PEELING GINGER The simplest way to peel ginger is to hold the ginger in one hand and drag the edge of a teaspoon across the surface to make the peel come off. As a tool, a spoon is easier and more efficient to use than a vegetable peeler or a knife and you'll have very little waste, as well.

CABBAGE
AND
LAMB CASSEROLE

In Sweden we have a classic cabbage-dish called *kåldolmar*, which is a classic "granny-dish" for me. So delicious and full of love, since it takes a while to make it. Here I speed it up a bit by making it as a casserole and exchanging the classic pork with lamb, which I think is really nice. Even if you don't think you're a cabbage or lamb fan, I think you'll be won over by this dish. Have it with a glass of good beer!

20 minutes + 40 minutes   ▪   4 servings

2¼ pounds (1 kg, 1 large head) white cabbage

3 tablespoons butter

¼ cup (60ml) apple cider vinegar

⅔ cup (1½dl) light corn syrup or golden syrup

Salt and white pepper

Lingonberry preserves

LAMB BLEND

3 tablespoons bread crumbs

2 tablespoons concentrated beef bouillon

1¼ cups (3dl) heavy cream

2 yellow onions

1⅓ pounds (600g) ground lamb

1½ tablespoons coarsely ground allspice

Salt and white pepper

1. Preheat the oven to 350°F (175°C). Coarsely shred the cabbage. Add the butter to a large saucepan and sauté the cabbage in batches until it begins to brown. Put all the cabbage back in the pan, add the vinegar and light corn (or golden) syrup to the pan, and let the liquid come to a boil. Season the mixture with salt and white pepper, and set it aside.

2. To make the lamb blend, mix the bread crumbs, bouillon, and cream in a large bowl and let it rest for about 5 minutes. Peel and finely chop the onions and add them to the bowl along with the ground lamb and allspice. Season the mixture with salt and white pepper, and work it together with your fingers or a fork to combine thoroughly.

3. Fold the cabbage into the ground meat mixture in the bowl. Spread the mixture into a casserole or baking dish. Place the dish on the middle rack of the oven and bake for about 40 minutes or until the top is a crisp golden brown. Serve with lingonberry preserves.

MACKEREL AND CHANTERELLE GRATIN

This is something for the cold weather! It includes just about every wintertime comfort food you can think of, too: cheese, potatoes, and mushrooms fried in fresh butter. Chanterelles add a unique flavor to the dish, but if none are available, you can use other mushrooms, such as cremini or porcini.

15 + 30 minutes ▪ 4 servings

7 ounces (200g) chanterelle mushrooms

3 tablespoons butter

Salt and white pepper

10 ounces (300g, about 2 large) peeled and boiled potatoes

1 6-inch (15-centimeter) leek

1 bunch flat-leaf parsley

400 g fresh mackerel filet, or fresh herring if you get a hold of it

3 tablespoons (50g) grated Parmesan cheese

¼ cups (3dl) heavy cream

1. Preheat the oven to 400°F (200°C). Rinse and drain the chanterelles on paper towels. Blot off any excess water. Add the butter to a medium-size frying pan or saucepan and fry the chanterelles in the butter until they're golden brown. Season them with a little salt. Cut the potatoes into thick slices. Slice the leek and carefully rinse it in cool water to remove any sand or grit. Finely chop the parsley.

2. With your fingers, roll up the mackerel fillets. Layer the potatoes, mackerel fillets cut in smaller pieces, leeks, mushrooms, parsley, and most of the cheese in a baking dish. Pour the cream over the top and sprinkle the remaining cheese on top.

3. Place the baking dish on the middle rack of the oven and bake the mixture for about 30 minutes or until it is golden brown. Let the gratin rest for 15–20 minutes before serving.

BACON AND ROASTED ROOT VEGETABLE "PANCAKE"

This is an unusual casserole that is more like a hearty, savory pancake than anything else. It's something I make a lot for my family, especially since we have hens at the farm. A mix of roasted root vegetables—carrots, turnips, parsnips (whatever you have on hand)—makes this a filling pancake. Just add onions and bacon to the veggies in the casserole and pour the pancake batter over the top. The result is an amazingly good pancake, perfect as a substantial snack or lunch.

15 minutes + 45 minutes ▪ 4–6 servings

BATTER

5 eggs

½ cup (1 dl) milk

5 cups flour

1 teaspoon salt

FILLING

14 ounces (400g) mixed root vegetables, such as carrots, turnips, parsnips, and celeriac (celery root)

1 red onion

1 white onion

5 ounces (150g, about 6 slices) smoked and cured bacon

2 tablespoons canola oil

Salt

TO SERVE

Lingonberry preserves

1. Preheat the oven to 450°F (225°C).

2. To make the batter for the "pancake": In a large bowl, whisk the eggs with a little of the milk. Gradually whisk the flour into the eggs and milk, until the batter is smooth. Pour in the rest of the milk and the salt. Mix well. Let the batter rest while you prepare and roast the root vegetables and bacon. (The longer you let the batter rest, the better. It will improve the quality of the pancake.)

3. To make the filling: Peel the vegetables and cut them into small pieces. Dice the onions coarsely. Dice the bacon. Put the vegetables, onions, and bacon in a large roasting pan, preferably with high sides, and toss with the oil. Season the mixture with salt. Place the tray on the middle rack of the oven and roast the veggie and bacon mixture for 15–20 minutes or until the vegetables are almost soft and the bacon is cooked.

4. Remove the casserole from the oven and carefully pour the pancake batter into the hot tray. Return the tray to the oven and roast the mixture for about 30 more minutes, or until the top is nicely browned. Serve the pancake warm with some Lingonberry preserves.

SHEPHERD'S PIE
WITH
SMOKED PORK SAUSAGE

Fans of smoked pork sausage, take note! This is one of my favorites, and I think it will warm your heart, too, especially when the weather turns cold. I often use a Swedish smoked sausage, which also has a somewhat sour flavor.

20 + about 25 minutes ■ 4 servings

TOPPING

1 pound (500g, about 3 large) potatoes

1 pound (500g, about 2 large) turnips

¼ cup (½dl) cream

1 egg yolk

2 tablespoons butter

¼ cup (50g) grated cheddar cheese

Salt and black pepper

FILLING

1½ yellow onions

6 large smoked fresh pork sausages

2 tablespoons butter

Salt and black pepper

6–8 whole pickled beets (see page 204)

1. Preheat the oven to 450°F (225°C). Peel the potatoes and turnips and cut them into small pieces. Put the vegetables in a large pot of salted water and boil them until they are soft.

2. In the meantime, prepare the filling: Peel and chop the onions. Slice the sausages, remove the sausage skins, and crumble the sausage with your fingers or the back of a spoon. Add the butter to a large saucepan and sauté the onion and sausage until sausage is cooked and the onions are soft. Season the mixture with salt and pepper. Coarsely chop the beets and add them to the pan. Spread the mixture evenly in a large baking dish or casserole.

3. Drain the boiled potatoes and turnips. Transfer them to a large bowl. Use a potato masher or a fork to mash the turnips with the potatoes, and then add the cream, egg yolk, and butter. With an electric hand mixer, puree the mixture (a few lumps are okay and add some nice texture). Stir in the cheese. Season with salt. Spread the mash over the sausage mixture in the casserole, and bake on the middle rack of the oven for 20–25 minutes or until the top turns golden brown. Serve with pickled beets, if you like.

OVEN-ROASTED ITALIAN SAUSAGE WITH TOMATOES AND FENNEL

This is perfect one-pot cooking. Everything goes into one pan, and then you pop it into the oven. The result is a lovely dish that evokes fond memories of lazy summer holidays in Italy. I like to serve it with a loaf of good, crusty bread, but if you want something even more filling, it is excellent with some freshly cooked pasta.

45 minutes ▪ 4 servings

2 red onions

2–3 cloves garlic

2 small fennel bulbs

1 pound (500g) good-quality sweet Italian sausage

½ red chile, such as Fresno, seeded

3 tablespoons olive oil

1 14-ounce can (400g) diced tomatoes

1 pinch of sugar

3 sprigs fresh rosemary

Salt and black pepper

Grated Parmesan cheese (optional)

1. Preheat the oven to 450°F (225°C). Peel and slice the onions and garlic. Clean and thinly slice the fennel. Slice the sausages once across the middle and then once lengthwise. Finely chop the chile.

2. Drizzle the olive oil into the baking dish and add the onions, garlic, fennel, sausages, and chile. Toss all the ingredients together and put the dish on a rack in the middle of the oven. Roast for about 15 minutes.

3. Stir the mixture and add the tomatoes, sugar, and rosemary sprigs. Roast for about 30 more minutes or until the sausage begins to turn a bit caramelized brown. Stir occasionally. Season with salt and pepper, and, if you like, some grated Parmesan cheese.

VEGGIE AND GORGONZOLA STEW

I feel completely energized whenever I dig into this hearty vegetable stew. The Gorgonzola adds both creaminess and a pleasant tang, and the stew also pairs nicely with some grilled chicken or good sausages, if you want to add some protein to the dish. It comes together quickly—perfect for those times when you need to power up but are pressed for time. If you're on a more leisurely schedule and are settling in for a quiet but productive evening, it wouldn't hurt to have a nice glass of red wine while the stew's in the oven.

15 + about 40 minutes ■ 4 servings

1¾ pounds (800g) potatoes

2 red bell peppers

1 large red onion

3 cloves garlic

½ red chile, such as Fresno, seeded

2 tablespoons olive oil

2 14-ounce (800g) cans diced tomatoes

½ teaspoon sugar

¼ cup (about 1 dl) chopped fresh oregano, plus extra for garnish

Salt and black pepper

FOR SERVING

4 ounces (130g, about ¼ cup) pitted black Kalamata olives

7 ounces (200g) Gorgonzola cheese

1. Preheat the oven to 450°F (225°C). Peel and cut the potatoes into thin slices. Seed the bell peppers and cut them into small pieces. Peel and slice the onion. Peel the garlic and chop it finely. Finely chop the chile.

2. Drizzle the olive oil into a casserole or a baking dish and add the potatoes, bell peppers, onion, garlic, chile, tomatoes, sugar, and oregano. Toss thoroughly and season with salt and pepper.

3. Put the dish on a rack in the middle of the oven and roast the stew for about 40 minutes or until the veggies are soft. Stir occasionally. Crumble the Gorgonzola into pieces and sprinkle it, along with the olives and extra oregano, on top of the veggies. Serve with plenty of good bread to soak up the delicious sauce.

COLD-WEATHER SOUPS

Pho with Pork, 86

Lentil and Roast Chicken Soup, 89

Chicken Tarragon Soup, 90

French Onion Soup, 93

Broccoli Soup with Blue Cheese, 94

Spanish Mussel Soup, 97

Mexican-Style Corn Soup, 98

Potage aux Légumes (Vegetable Soup), 101

Creamy Potato and Bean Soup, 102

Minestrone with Prosciutto and Angel Hair Pasta, 105

I'm a soup person. From light noodle, filling potato or bean, and rich meat soups to all kinds of everything-but-the-kitchen sink, use-what-you-have home-style recipes—I love them all! And, as you'll see from the ingredient lists in this chapter, all you need is a little imagination and, on occasion, a few additions to your shopping list (maybe some fresh mint, a couple of limes, or a knob of ginger)—to give a winter soup, whether it's meat- or vegetable-based, a little extra boost of bright flavor and the promise of warmer days to come.

You'll also discover that it doesn't take much—in fact, you don't need many ingredients at all, least of all exotic or out-of-season ones, to make a great soup. Sometimes all you need is 15 minutes, some onions, a dash of wine, and a little chicken broth to make something special.

PHO WITH PORK

In Vietnam, this aromatic noodle soup is served for breakfast and lunch as well as for dinner. Opt for meat in whole pieces and preferably with the bones for a stronger flavor. When serving, pull apart the meat into smaller pieces. Or skip the meat completely! You can even cook the broth in advance.

About 20 minutes + 1 ½ hour ▪ 4 servings

BROTH

2 large yellow onions

2 cloves garlic

½ red chile, such as Fresno, seeded

2 large (350g) carrots

3-inch piece (50g) fresh ginger

2 tablespoons cooking oil

8 cloves

2 cinnamon sticks

4 star anise pods

1½ quarts (1½ liters) beef or vegetable broth, maybe more

¼ cup (½dl) fish sauce

1¾ pounds (800g) bone-in pork loin chops

Salt (optional)

FOR SERVING

10 ounces (300g) wide rice noodles

¼ head iceberg lettuce

6 scallions

½ bunch fresh mint

2 stalks Thai basil

½ bunch fresh cilantro

1 red chile, such as Fresno, seeded

4 ounces (100g, about 1 cup) mung bean sprouts

Hoisin sauce

Fish sauce

Chili sauce

GARNISH

3–4 tablespoons fried garlic or roasted onions (optional)

1. Peel and roughly chop the onions and garlic. Coarsely chop the chile. Peel the carrots and grate them coarsely. Peel and finely chop the ginger (see peeling tips on page 68).

2. Add the oil to a large soup pot or saucepan and sauté the onion, garlic, carrots, ginger, chile, cloves, cinnamon, and anise for a few minutes. Add the broth, fish sauce, and pork and bring to a boil. Let the mixture simmer over low heat for 1–1½ hours covered, or until the meat is tender and pulls away from the bone. Taste the broth and add some salt, if needed. Remove the meat from the pot, pull it apart into small pieces, and set it aside.

3. Cook the rice noodles according to directions on package. Shred the iceberg lettuce and coarsely slice the scallions. Coarsely chop the mint, basil, and cilantro. Finely chop the chile. Add all these ingredients to the soup bowls, along with the mung bean sprouts.

4. Fill the bowls with the broth and meat. Garnish the soup with fried garlic or some roasted onion on top, if you like, and serve immediately. Pass around hoisin sauce, fish sauce, and chili sauce, and let folks help themselves.

LENTIL
AND
ROAST CHICKEN SOUP

Making soup with red lentils is actually a bit like making something out of nothing. You may start out with a bit of a watery broth, but when you add the lentils and cook the mix a little longer...presto! You have a hearty, super-wholesome, and amazingly delicious soup to slurp.

It's pure magic! Even more magical: You don't have to take the time to roast your own chicken. A store-bought rotisserie chicken will do the trick.

25 minutes ▪ 4 servings

2 yellow onions

2 cloves garlic

1 red chile, such as Fresno, seeded

1 tablespoon cooking oil

1 teaspoon ground cumin

1 teaspoon ground coriander

1 14-ounce can (400g) crushed tomatoes

1 quart (1 liter) chicken or vegetable broth

1 cup (2½dl) red lentils

Salt and black pepper

Freshly squeezed lime juice (optional)

FOR SERVING
Meat from ½ roasted chicken

1–2 avocados, peeled and sliced

4 ounces (125g) fresh mozzarella

1. Peel and finely chop the onions and garlic. Finely chop the chile.

2. Add the oil to a soup pot and sauté the onion, garlic, and chile until the onion is soft. Add the cumin and coriander to the mix and sauté them for a few minutes. Increase the heat, pour in the crushed tomatoes and cook them for a couple of minutes. Stir in the chicken broth. Bring the mixture to a boil and let it cook over high heat, uncovered, for about 5 minutes. Add the lentils, stir, and reduce heat. Let the soup simmer for about 15 minutes, or until the lentils are soft. Stir occasionally. Add more broth if the liquid cooks down too much.

3. Season the soup with salt and pepper and, if you like, a squeeze of lime juice. Serve the soup topped with chicken meat, avocado slices, and some mozzarella. Be generous with the toppings!

CHICKEN TARRAGON SOUP

This is such a good recipe that it would be almost criminal not to share it. It's perfect for gray autumn or winter days when you might be feeling a little down. Catch a cold, and you're right in the thick of it. This soup is so smooth, warm, and good that it will immediately raise your spirits. Sometimes I purée it into a smooth soup, after removing the chicken, and sometimes I just serve it as it is. Delicious!

About 35 minutes ■ 4 servings

1 yellow onion
2 cloves garlic
½ small leek
2 celery stalks
1 tablespoon olive oil
1¾ pounds (800g) bone-in chicken pieces
1¼ cups (3dl) unoaked, dry white wine
½ tablespoons dried tarragon
2½ cups (6dl) chicken broth
¾ cup (2dl) heavy cream
2 teaspoons white wine vinegar
Salt and black pepper

1. Peel and finely chop the onion and garlic. Slice the leek and carefully rinse it to remove any sand or grit. Dry off the slices with a clean kitchen towel or paper towels. Slice the celery.

2. Add the olive oil to a large soup pot and gently fry the onion, garlic, and leek. Add the celery, chicken, wine, tarragon, broth, cream, and vinegar, and bring to a boil. Simmer the soup over medium heat, until the chicken is thoroughly cooked, about 30 minutes.

3. Remove the chicken from the pot and pick the meat off the bones. Return the meat to the soup, season it with salt and pepper, and serve with a loaf of good bread.

FRENCH ONION SOUP

How is it possible for anyone to get through dark, cold autumn or winter days without eating some type of cheese-topped onion soup? Thank heaven the French have invented just the thing. The ingredients for this heavenly soup are inexpensive, and the broth is ridiculously good and so easy to make that you can do it with your hands tied behind you—if someone else chops the onion, that is. Otherwise, you can have a good cry while you chop all the onions, which might be just what you need! In any event, choose a flavorful and high-fat cheese for the gratin, Gruyere is always nice, and remember that you really don't need to burn the onion. Low heat and patience, my friend . . . patience. Vive la France!

About 1 hour ▪ 4 servings

8 yellow onions

2 cloves garlic

2 small tart apples

¼ cup (50g) butter

1 tablespoon dried (or 3 fresh twigs) thyme

1 pinch of sugar

1¼ cups (3dl) unoaked, dry white wine

3¾ cups (9dl) chicken or vegetable broth

Salt and black pepper

4–8 slices light sourdough bread

4 ounces (120g, about 1 cup) aged cheese, such as cheddar or Gruyère, grated

1. Preheat the oven to 450°F (225°C). Peel and finely chop the onions and garlic. Peel, core, and finely chop the apples.

2. In a large pot, slowly melt the butter. Add the onion and garlic and sauté gently over low heat. The onions should not have any color at all; they should just look smooth and glossy. Add the apple, thyme, sugar, wine, and broth, and bring to a boil. Let the soup simmer for about 20 minutes without a lid. Season with salt and pepper.

3. If you like, cut the crusts off the bread. Divide the soup into four ovenproof bowls. Place a slice of bread atop each bowl and finish with a generous sprinkling of grated cheese. Place the bowls on the middle rack of the oven and bake for about 15 minutes or until the cheese begins to turn golden brown. Serve immediately.

BROCCOLI SOUP WITH BLUE CHEESE

I don't know about you, but I love broccoli. When I was pregnant, I had cravings for steamed broccoli with Parmesan cheese and hazelnut oil. Broccoli tastes especially good with cheese and nutty flavors, and you can definitely taste them in this lightning-fast and creamy soup, if you finish it, as I do, with a good blue cheese and salty roasted almonds.

30 minutes ▪ 4 servings

8 ounces (250g, about 3 cups) broccoli, trimmed stalks and florets

½ leek

2 cloves garlic

2 tablespoons cooking oil

3 cups (8dl) chicken or vegetable broth

¾ cup (2dl) crème fraîche

Salt and black pepper

1½ cups (200g) frozen green peas

2 tablespoons chopped dill

Zest of 1 lemon (preferably organic)

2 teaspoons lemon juice

¼ cup (50g) salted roasted almonds, coarsely chopped

4 ounces (125g) blue cheese

1. Cut the broccoli into small pieces (both florets and stalk). Slice the leek and carefully rinse it to remove any sand or grit. Peel and chop the garlic.
2. Add the oil to a soup pot and sauté the leeks and garlic together for a couple of minutes. Add the broccoli, broth, and crème fraîche. Season with salt and pepper. Bring to a boil, and simmer uncovered until the broccoli is soft. Add the peas and dill and cook for just a couple of minutes.
3. Using an immersion blender, process the soup until it is completely smooth. Add the lemon zest and juice. Salt and pepper to taste. Serve the soup topped with coarsely chopped salted roasted almonds and blue cheese broken into small pieces.

NOTE It's easy to make your own pan-roasted salted almonds. Just pour a little olive oil into a large heavy frying pan (a cast iron skillet is ideal), making sure to thoroughly coat the bottom of the pan. Spread the almonds evenly over the surface and cook them over medium-high heat for a couple of minutes, or until they start to color and become fragrant. Stir the almonds, sprinkle a little salt (sea salt, if you have some in the pantry) over them, stir again, and continue to cook the almonds, stirring them every 30 seconds or so, until they become brown and toasty, about 5 minutes.

SPANISH MUSSEL SOUP

Mussels are fantastic fast food and actually one of the most common things I cook when I throw a big dinner! Buy a couple of buckets of them from your local fishmonger, throw them into a pot with some wine, veggies, cream, and chorizo (the "Spanish" element in this mix), and you have a fine mussel soup in no time. This, good people, may well be the simplest recipe in the book

30 minutes ■ 4-6 servings

2 buckets, about 4 pounds (2kg) fresh mussels

2 yellow onions

3 cloves garlic

½ red chile, such as Fresno, seeded

2 large carrots (250g)

3 fresh chorizo sausages

2 tablespoons olive oil

2–2½ tablespoons smoked paprika

2 cups (4½dl) unoaked, dry white wine

2 cups (4½dl) cream

½ sprig fresh thyme, leaves only

Salt and black pepper

1. Place the mussels in a large bowl and rinse them thoroughly under running cold water for about 5 minutes to get rid of any sand or grit. Discard any broken mussels. Using a sharp paring knife, scrape off the "beard" that sometimes grows along the edges of the shell.

2. Peel and finely chop the onions and garlic. Finely chop the chile. Peel and finely dice the carrots. Cut the sausage into thin slices. Add the olive oil to a deep pot and sauté the onion, garlic, and chile until the onion has become soft. Add the paprika, carrots, and sausage to the pot and sear the sausage until it turns a burnished red-brown.

3. Raise the temperature to maximum heat, add the mussels, and cover the pot. Let everything cook thoroughly for about 2–3 minutes, stirring occasionally. Add the wine, cream, and thyme and cook for another 5 minutes over high heat. Remove the pot from the stove and discard any mussels that did not open. Season the soup with salt and pepper. Serve with a loaf of excellent crusty bread and some nice wine or beer.

MEXICAN-STYLE CORN SOUP

I love how you can make a wonderfully creamy soup without the use of dairy products, thanks to corn. Toasting the kernels really brings out an amazing flavor and gives this soup its beautiful color. It you want to add extra creaminess and texture, top it off with a mixture of grated feta cheese and shredded mozzarella. The jalapeño adds just enough heat to warm you up without burning down the house. Toast some tortillas to serve with the soup, and if you have any cold beer, now's the time to take it out of the fridge and fill a glass for yourself and your guests.

About 25 minutes ■ 4 servings

2 yellow onions

2 large cloves garlic

1 large fresh jalapeño

2 tablespoons cooking oil

2½ cups (420 grams) fresh corn kernels, cut off the cob (or thawed frozen or drained canned corn kernels)

3⅓ cups (8dl) chicken or vegetable broth

3 teaspoons ground cumin

Juice of 1 lime

Salt and black pepper

1. Peel and finely chop the onions and garlic. Finely chop the jalapeño. Add the oil to a large pot and add the corn kernels. Roast them over high heat for 5–7 minutes or until the kernels turn golden and are flecked with brown. Stir the corn frequently to keep it from burning.

2. Add the onion, garlic, and jalapeño to the pot, and sauté until the onions have become soft. Stir in the broth and the cumin, and bring the mixture to a boil. Simmer, uncovered, for about 15 minutes.

3. Using an immersion blender, process the soup until it's smooth or semi-smooth if you like a bit of texture, and season it with lime juice and salt and pepper. Serve the soup with a sprinkling of fresh cilantro leaves on top and toasted tortillas on the side.

POTAGE AUX LÉGUMES (VEGETABLE SOUP)

To bring out the French in you, pour yourself a glass of red wine and get started on this hearty, French-inspired soup. The longer it simmers on the stove, the better it gets. The trick is to keep adding the broth slowly, as the vegetables cook in the pot. I've used candy-striped beets in this recipe, but it tastes just as delicious with other root vegetables—or why not try pumpkin?

About 35 minutes ▪ 4 servings

2 yellow onions

2 large cloves garlic

½ red chile, such as Fresno, seeded

¼ cup (50g) butter

14 ounces (400g, about 3 large) potatoes

3 large (300g) carrots

10 ounces (300g, about 2 large) candy-striped beets or red beets

2 teaspoons dried thyme

8 large sage leaves

¾ cup (2dl) unoaked, dry white wine

3½ cups (8dl) chicken or vegetable broth

Salt and black pepper

1. Peel and chop the onions and garlic. Chop the chile. Peel the potatoes, carrots, and beets, and cut them into rough, uniform-size pieces.

2. Melt the butter in a large pot and sauté the onion, garlic, and chile until the onion is soft. Add the potatoes, carrots, beets, thyme, sage, wine, and a little of the broth just so it covers the veggies. Bring the mixture to a boil and simmer, covered, until the vegetables are soft. Stir often and add the rest of the broth little by little, just as you would when cooking a risotto (see the example on page 117).

3. Mash some of the vegetables with a potato masher to make the soup a little thicker, if you like. Taste the soup and add salt and pepper and possibly a little more broth (if the soup seems too thick). Serve it piping hot with grated Parmesan cheese on top and good rustic bread on the side.

CREAMY POTATO
AND
BEAN SOUP

The potato is a starchy root vegetable, and putting it in a soup is a smart way to achieve a richer texture. Here I cook potatoes and beans together for a really wholesome and tasty soup. This is the kind of stick-to-the-ribs soup you want to serve on a particularly cold winter evening—or for lunch—when you have to do some heavy work outside, like shoveling more snow.

About 25 minutes ■ 4 servings

1 yellow onion

2 large cloves garlic

1 pound (500g) potatoes

2 tablespoons olive oil

1½ teaspoons dried thyme

2 cups (5dl) vegetable broth

¾ cup (2dl) crème fraîche

¼ cup (3dl) milk

1 14-ounce can (400g) white beans

Salt and black pepper

TO SERVE

Smoked white fish

good olive oil

1. Peel and chop the onion and garlic. Peel the potatoes and cut them into small pieces.

2. Add the olive oil to a soup pot or large saucepan and gently sauté the onions and garlic. Add the potatoes, thyme, broth, crème fraîche, and milk. Season the mixture with salt and pepper and bring it to a boil. Boil uncovered for about 10 minutes, and then add the beans. Cook until the potatoes are soft, then process the mixture with an immersion blender until it is smooth.

3. Season the soup with salt and pepper, to taste, and then serve the soup topped with bits of smoked fish, if you like (I like smoked whitefish), and some good olive oil swirled on top.

MINESTRONE
WITH
PROSCIUTTO AND
ANGEL HAIR PASTA

Who hasn't been served a tired minestrone: watery tomato soup with overcooked beans and macaroni that falls apart? We've all been there, and that's too bad, because when it's handled with respect, classic minestrone can be a supergood soup. Here, I skip the tomatoes and beans and replace them with chicken broth and prosciutto. I also use capellini (angel hair pasta) instead of the usual shell pasta or macaroni to give the soup a pleasant lightness.

25 minutes ■ 4 servings

7 ounces (200g) prosciutto, cut into thick slices

2 medium (200g) carrots

2 yellow onions

2 large cloves garlic

½ red chile, such as Fresno, seeded

2 tablespoons olive oil

⅔ cup (1½dl) chicken broth

6 ounces (180g) angel hair or other thin spaghetti

Salt and black pepper

Handful of fresh mint leaves, minced or coarsely chopped

1. Dice the prosciutto. Peel and cut the carrots into small cubes, about ¼ inch (5mm). Peel and chop the onions and garlic. Chop the chile.

2. Add the olive oil to a soup pot or large saucepan and fry the prosciutto, carrot, onion, garlic, and chile over medium heat until the onion is soft. Add the broth and bring the mixture to a boil. Boil, covered, for about 15 minutes over medium heat. Break the spaghetti in half once and add it to the pot. Cook the soup for about 3 minutes or until the pasta is al dente.

3. Season the soup with salt and pepper and serve it topped with fresh mint leaves.

RICE AND PASTA SPECIALS

Fried Rice with Cauliflower and Sesame, 110

Creamy Carbonara with Pork Belly and Peas, 113

Pasta with Kale Sautéed in Garlic and Pecorino, 114

Rye Risotto with Oyster Mushrooms Sautéed
  in Butter, 117

Russian Beef Hash with Beets and Pickles, 118

Paella with a Twist, 121

Paella on the Grill, 122

Mac and Cheese, 125

Pasta alla Puttanesca, 126

Pumpkin Risotto with Fried Sage, 129

Two-Day Bolognese, 130

Risotto with Bacon and Mushrooms, 133

A really good pasta works like a balm for the soul. It softens hard edges, transforms the everyday into party fare, and keeps things going when the winter seems especially dark. And as far as tools go, it couldn't be easier to make the recipes in this chapter. All you need is a large pot, a big wooden spoon for stirring, and last but not least, a good grater for zesting lemons and grating Parmesan cheese and garlic.

Whether it's pasta with a rich Bolognese sauce or a homey risotto with bacon and mushrooms, you'll find recipes that are easy to make and quick to satisfy wintertime cravings for comfort and warmth. And, if you want a break from rich meat sauces, definitely try Pumpkin Risotto with Fried Sage (see page 129). It's incredibly good. You'll also find that the recipes in this chapter are versatile and easy to change up, depending on what you have in the fridge or larder. And if all your kids want to eat is mac and cheese, no problem—go straight to page 125 and enjoy!

FRIED RICE WITH CAULIFLOWER AND SESAME

What *is* it that makes fried rice so great? The answer depends on whom you ask—but if you ask me, the answer is well-fried rice that achieves a fine, slightly nutty flavor. And the rice definitely has to be cooled completely before use, so I prefer to cook it the day before. And rather than scrambling the eggs first, I prefer to stir them into the rice, which makes it wonderfully moist and lush.

30 minutes ▪ 4 servings

1¼ cups (3dl) jasmine rice

2 medium (200g) carrots

3-inch piece (50g) fresh ginger

1 red chile, such as Fresno, seeded

6 scallions

2 tablespoons cooking oil

2 cups (300g) cauliflower florets

2 tablespoons sesame oil

¼ cup (½dl) light Japanese soy sauce

2 tablespoons oyster sauce

¼ cup (½dl) toasted sesame seeds

4 eggs

Juice from 1 lime

Handful of fresh cilantro for garnish

1. Cook the jasmine rice according to the directions on the package and let it cool. Peel and finely grate the carrots. Peel and finely chop the ginger (see peeling tips on page 68) and finely chop the chile. Slice the scallions and set them aside.

2. Add the oil to a wok or large frying pan. Stir-fry the carrots, ginger, chile, and cauliflower over very high heat, stirring constantly until the vegetables begin to soften a little but still have some crispness. Push the vegetables to one side of the pan, and add the cooked rice. Keep the pan over high heat, stirring occasionally until the rice begins to turn golden brown.

3. Stir the vegetables and the rice together in the pan and add the sesame oil, soy sauce, oyster sauce, and sesame seeds. Mix thoroughly, while keeping the pan over very high heat. Then add the eggs to the rice, one at a time, stirring the mixture to thoroughly incorporate the eggs into the rice. Season with lime juice, garnish with scallions and cilantro, and serve immediately with more soy sauce on the side.

> **NOTE** Before frying the rice, cook it and let it cool. For some inexplicable reason, it just tastes better that way.

CREAMY CARBONARA WITH PORK BELLY AND PEAS

I like the smooth creaminess of this variation on the classic recipe for carbonara. The peas and chives give the dish a fresh taste, while the fried pork belly adds a welcome smokiness.

About 20 minutes ▪ 4 servings

1 pound (500g) pasta, preferably tagliatelle, linguini, or spaghetti

1 onion

2 cloves of garlic

1–2 tablespoons olive oil for frying

7 ounces (200g) salted pork belly

1¾ cups (4dl) green peas, frozen and thawed

4 egg yolks

⅔ cup (1½dl) heavy cream

1¼–1¾ cups (4dl) finely grated Parmesan cheese

⅔ cup (1½dl) finely chopped chives

Salt and plenty of freshly ground black pepper

Arugula leaves, for garnish (optional)

1. Cook the pasta al dente in salted water. Chop the onion and the garlic. Meanwhile, add the olive oil to a large frying pan or saucepan, preferably with high sides. Chop and fry the pork belly until it browns nicely and crisps up. Add the thawed peas to warm them through.

2. In a bowl, stir together the egg yolks, cream, ⅔ of the Parmesan, and all the chives. Add about ½ cup of the pasta water to the pan. This will act as a starchy liquid. Drain the freshly cooked pasta and fold it into the pan with the pork belly and peas. Pour in the egg mixture. Remove the pan from the heat and gently toss everything until it is well mixed. Season with salt and plenty of black pepper. Top with the remaining Parmesan and serve immediately, preferably with a scattering of fresh arugula leaves on top.

PASTA WITH KALE SAUTÉED IN GARLIC AND PECORINO

Here you get the best of both worlds: comforting pasta (a carb I crave, especially when it's cold!) plus the robust, bright flavor of kale (it's packed with vitamins, minerals, and fiber—facts that will make you feel better about that second helping of pasta). Lemon juice and lemon zest add a fresh zing that compliments the kale, and there's a nice crunch factor, too, from the toasty, garlicky croutons.

About 30 minutes ▪ 4 servings

1 pound (500g) pasta

1 onion

3 cloves garlic

⅓ red chile, such as Fresno, seeded

3 end slices of day-old light bread

10 ounces (300g, about 1 bunch) lacinato (also known as cavolo nero ["black cabbage"] and dinosaur) kale

2 tablespoons olive oil, divided

Salt and black pepper

2 teaspoons lemon juice

2 tablespoons butter

Zest of 1½ lemons

3 tablespoons (50g) toasted pine nuts

Finely grated Pecorino cheese

1. Cook the pasta al dente in salted water (save a little of the cooking water). In the meantime, chop onion, garlic, and chile. Add the bread to a food processor and pulse it (or chop it by hand) to make small crumbs. Cut the coarse stems from the kale and slice the leaves.

2. Pour half the olive oil into a large frying pan or saucepan and fry the bread crumbs and half the garlic until golden brown. Season the mixture with salt and pepper. Transfer the garlicky bread crumbs to a plate and set it aside. Pour the rest of the olive oil into the pan and sauté the onion until it's soft. Add the kale and sauté until soft. Add the rest of the garlic and the chile and sauté for just a few minutes. Season with the lemon juice and salt and pepper. Toss the mix with some of the cooking water to make a little sauce in the pan. Spoon in the butter and whisk it in to enrich the sauce.

3. Mix the kale mixture with the pasta, lemon zest, bread crumbs, pine nuts, and a generous amount of Pecorino. Serve immediately

RYE RISOTTO WITH OYSTER MUSHROOMS SAUTÉED IN BUTTER

I used rye berries the first time I made this risotto, which gave it a pleasing, chewy texture, but cracked rye is easier to obtain and makes for a somewhat smoother risotto. If you can get your hands on rye berries, though, do give it a try. The hearty flavor of the grain, with its slight bitterness, pairs nicely with aged Cheddar or Parmesan cheese in this recipe. I use beer to get a slightly more malty taste, but if you like, you can use white wine, which works just as well—just leave out the vinegar. The trick with risotto is to keep an eye on it while you stir and add liquid to the pan. Your patience will be well rewarded.

About 30 minutes ▪ 4 servings

1 large yellow onion, chopped

1 large clove garlic, chopped

2 tablespoons butter for sautéing, plus 5 teaspoons for brown butter, divided

1¾ cups (4dl) cut or cracked rye

1¼ cups (3dl) light lager beer (or white wine)

¼ cup (½dl) apple cider vinegar

3⅓ cups (8dl) chicken broth

Salt and freshly ground black pepper

14 ounces (400g) oyster mushrooms (or other mushrooms)

1–2 cloves garlic

¾ cup (2dl) finely grated aged Parmesan or Cheddar cheese, plus additional for garnish

⅔ cup (1½dl) finely chopped parsley

1. Add 2 tablespoons of butter to a large saucepan and gently sauté the chopped onion and garlic. Add the rye and continue to sauté for a few minutes while stirring. Pour in the beer and vinegar (if you use wine, do not add the vinegar) and continue to cook over medium heat. Add some of the broth and cook on medium heat. Stir occasionally. Continue to add the broth gradually as the liquid cooks down. Continue to cook the mixture, stirring it periodically, until the rye starts to become al dente. Season with salt and pepper, and cook a few more minutes, until most of the broth has been absorbed by the grain.

2. Remove the pan from the heat when the rye is perfectly al dente—tender, with a little firmness at the center. By now the risotto should be quite loose and runny. Cover the pan and set it aside while you sauté the mushrooms.

3. Cut or break the mushrooms into pieces and chop the garlic. In a small saucepan, sauté the mushrooms in the remaining butter for "brown butter" until they are almost golden brown. Then add the garlic, season with salt and pepper, and sauté until the garlic is soft. Let the butter get brown.

4. Gently heat the risotto, if it has cooled, and add more liquid if it has become sticky. Add the cheese and stir until the cheese has melted and the rye feels creamy. Serve immediately with the mushrooms, chopped parsley, and grated Parmesan on top.

RUSSIAN BEEF HASH
WITH
BEETS AND PICKLES

This dish is a bit of a mash-up of classic Swedish hash and other ingredients, like red beets and pickles, which give the mix a Russian cast. Regardless, it is a dish that comes straight from my childhood. Sometimes I serve the hash with the eggs sunny side up or with a raw egg yolk, depending on what my guests prefer. If you love pickled beets as much as I do, this is a dish for you, and if you love beef hash, try this one. The beets and pickles really do add something special to the dish, and you can't beat the color.

30 minutes   ■   4 servings

¾ cup (2dl) parboiled rice

Beef stock

2 yellow onions

2 tablespoons cooking oil

1 pound (500g) ground beef

2 tablespoons Dijon mustard or your choice of hot mustard

1¼ cups (3dl) finely chopped pickled beets

1½ cups finely chopped gherkins or dill pickles

3–4 tablespoons small capers or large chopped capers

¼ cup (½dl) pickling juice from the red beets

Salt and white pepper

FOR SERVING

4 egg yolks (for eating raw)

Large or small capers

1. Cook the rice in the beef stock according to the instructions on the package.

2. Peel and chop the onions. Add the oil to a large pot or saucepan and sauté the onions until they become soft. Add the ground beef to the pan and sear it until beef is cooked. Stir in the mustard, beets, pickles, capers, beet juice, and the cooked rice. Fry the mixture for about 3–5 minutes, stirring occasionally.

3. Season the hash with salt and pepper and plate each dish with a raw egg yolk and capers.

NOTE Eating raw or undercooked eggs can pose a health risk, especially to the elderly, young children under the age of four, pregnant women, and other highly susceptible individuals with compromised immune systems. Make sure that foods that contain raw or lightly cooked eggs are made only with pasteurized eggs. Cooking eggs reduces the risk of illness.

PAELLA with a TWIST

Paella, a classic Spanish dish, is traditionally made with rice, but here I've given it an Italian twist and replaced the rice with orzo, a short-cut pasta that actually looks like a large grain of rice. Paella is incredibly versatile and enjoyed all over the world. It is prepared with a wide variety of ingredients, such as seafood, seasonal vegetables, beans, and meats, along with the bright orange-yellow saffron-scented rice that has made this dish so recognizable almost anywhere you go. My version is a savory mix of veggies, chicken, chorizo, white beans, saffron, and beer—a real fall and winter favorite!

About 40 minutes ▪ 4 servings

1 large yellow onion

2 cloves garlic

1 red chile, such as Fresno, seeded

2 red bell peppers

1⅓ pounds (600g) boneless chicken legs

7 ounces (200g) dried chorizo

½ cup (1 dl) olive oil

1 teaspoon saffron threads

1½ tablespoons smoked paprika

1 14-ounce can (400g) diced tomatoes

2 cups (5 dl) lager (beer)

1½–2 cups (4–5dl) chicken broth

1 14-ounce can (400g) white beans

14 ounces (400g) orzo

Salt and black pepper

Freshly squeezed lemon juice

FOR SERVING

Kalamata olives, pitted and coarsely chopped

Parsley, chopped

1. Peel and finely chop the onion and garlic. Finely chop the chile. Seed the bell peppers and cut them into small pieces. Cut the chicken into pieces. Cut the chorizo into thick slices.

2. Add the olive oil to a large pot or saucepan and brown the chicken. Add the onion, garlic, and chile, and sauté until the onion is soft. Stir in the saffron, paprika, chorizo, and peppers, and fry for about a minute, while continuing to stir. Add the tomatoes, beer, and some of the chicken broth (just so it covers) to the pan and bring the mixture to a boil on medium-high.

3. Let the paella simmer on low heat until the liquid has cooked down, and the chicken is completely cooked through, about 20 minutes. Continue to add more broth, so it just covers the mixture. Drain the beans and stir them into the paella, add some more broth, add the orzo, and let cook for about 8–10 minutes, adding more broth when needed. Stir the mixture now and then, but not too often.

4. Season the paella with salt, pepper, and lemon juice. Serve with pitted, coarsely chopped Kalamata olives and chopped parsley.

PAELLA ON THE GRILL

Not much beats a roaring fire, a large cook pot, and a big ladle—everything you need to make a phenomenal paella—in summer or in winter. Just remember to prep everything you need for the cook pot (or paella pan) and bring it with you as you head outdoors to get your coals going. You don't want to keep running back and forth to the house. If, however, you end up cooking the paella on the stove, it will be just as good—or almost as good—without the inimitable taste of the grill . . . and smoke, which makes everything taste better, no matter what it is.

40 minutes ■ 6 servings

2 yellow onions

2 large cloves garlic

½ red chile, such as Fresno, seeded

1 yellow bell pepper

1 red bell pepper

½–⅔ cup (1–1½dl) olive oil

1 fresh chicken (cut into pieces) or 1⅓ pounds (600g) boneless chicken thighs

1 teaspoon saffron threads

2 tablespoons smoked paprika

1¾ cups (4dl) Arborio rice

1 14-ounce can (400g) diced tomatoes

12 ounces (3dl) lager beer

1 quart (1 liter) chicken broth

Juice of 1 lemon

Salt and black pepper

¾ cup (125g) green peas (frozen and thawed)

8 ounces (250g) peeled shrimp, cooked (can be fresh or frozen and thawed)

1. Peel and finely chop the onions and garlic. Finely chop the chile. Core and cut the bell peppers into small pieces. Set a pot that can withstand high heat on the grill rack (or use a 20-inch paella pan over a standard 22-inch kettle grill) above hot briquettes and pour in ½ cup (1 dl) of the olive oil. Add the chicken pieces to the pot and sear them. Then add the onion, garlic, chile, smoked paprika, and saffron and let it cook for a bit while stirring. Add the rice and peppers and fry for another minute while stirring (add more oil, if the pan is dry). Stir in the diced tomatoes, beer, and chicken broth just so it covers. Gradually add more chicken broth at intervals, as the liquid boils down. Try not to stir too often.

2. Allow the rice mixture to cook until the chicken is done and the rice is soft. This takes about 25 minutes. Season the mixture with the lemon juice, salt, and pepper, and stir in the peas and the shrimp just before serving, making sure that they're warmed through.

3. Serve the paella creamy and piping hot.

NOTE Heat the broth on the stove and put it in an insulated vacuum bottle to keep it warm while you cook outside, so that you don't cool the paella every time you add broth.

MAC AND CHEESE

Macaroni and cheese has gotten a bad rap for being full of carbs and too much fat from butter, cheese, and cream, but the fact is you can make really good mac and cheese that will even get your kids' stamp of approval by using less (and less fatty) cheese along with healthy ingredients, like fresh cherry tomatoes. In fact, you can add just about any vegetable to this recipe—whatever you have in the house—including cooked root veggies, like butternut squash. Don't be shy about using other cheeses, too. Instead of feta, try ricotta. Yum.

About 45 minutes ■ 4 servings

14 ounces (400g) dried pasta shells

1 large yellow onion

2 cloves garlic

2 tablespoons olive oil

1 cup (250g) cherry tomatoes

¾ cup (2dl) heavy cream

10 ounces (300g, 2¼ cups) crumbled feta cheese

5 ounces (150g, 1½ cups) grated Parmesan cheese

Salt and black pepper

1. Preheat the oven to 450°F (225°C). Cook the pasta al dente in salted water as directed on the package. Drain the pasta. Peel and slice the onion. Peel and finely chop the garlic.

2. Add the olive oil to large saucepan and sauté the onion and garlic until the onion is soft. Add the cherry tomatoes to the pan cook them for a couple of minutes. Pour in the cream, feta, and Parmesan. Bring the mixture to a boil, while stirring, and season with salt and pepper. Add the pasta to the pan and then divide the mixture into four ovenproof individual ramekins or a large, wide baking dish.

3. Place the dishes on the middle rack of the oven and bake for about 25 minutes or until the cheese has turned golden brown.

PASTA ALLA PUTTANESCA

This spicy, fragrant pasta dish is said to have originated in the brothels of Naples, back in the day, as a quick dish that could easily be made from just a few ingredients—and in between customers. In addition to the tomatoes that you find in traditional tomato sauces, the garlic, capers, olives, anchovies, and black pepper puttanesca make a sauce that beautifully balances salty, sweet, and spicy elements. Here, the pasta is cooked directly in the sauce, which means that you may need to add a little more liquid to the mix than you might ordinarily use. If you boil the pasta in water, simply drain the pasta and mix it into the puttanesca sauce.

About 25 minutes ▪ 4 servings

1½ regular onions

3 cloves garlic

½ red chile, such as Fresno, seeded

4 ounces (130g, about ¼ cup) pitted Kalamata olives

12 small anchovy fillets

½ cup small capers

3 tablespoons olive oil

1 14-ounce can (400g) crushed tomatoes

2 cups (5dl) water

Salt and black pepper

1 pound (500g) fresh or dried tagliatelle, or any other ribbon pasta, like fettuccini or pappardelle

FOR SERVING

Grated Parmesan cheese

Coarsely chopped parsley

black pepper

1. Peel and slice the onion. Peel and finely chop the garlic. Finely chop the chile, olives, and anchovies. Chop the capers coarsely.

2. Add the olive oil to a large pot or saucepan and sauté the onion, garlic, and chile until the onion is soft. Add the olives, anchovies, and capers and sauté for a couple of minutes. Stir in the crushed tomatoes and water and bring to a boil. Cook the mixture over medium heat for about 10 minutes and season with salt and pepper. Add the pasta to the sauce. Let the mixture simmer, covered, on low heat until the pasta is cooked al dente. Stir the sauce occasionally, and add more water if necessary.

3. Sprinkle the pasta with lots of Parmesan and parsley, and serve immediately.

PUMPKIN RISOTTO WITH FRIED SAGE

I add the pumpkin to the mix early on so that it almost dissolves into the risotto, adding even more lushness to the dish. If you swap in squash for the pumpkin, try butternut squash. It's a little firmer than pumpkin and holds its shape a little better—and it's insanely good. No matter what you choose, you'll end up with an incredibly tasty risotto.

About 40 minutes ▪ 4 servings

1⅓ pounds (600g) pumpkin or butternut squash

1 large yellow onion

2 large cloves garlic

2 tablespoons olive oil

1 tablespoon dried thyme

1¼ cups (3dl) carnaroli (or Arborio) rice

1¼ cups (3dl) unoaked, dry white wine

1½ quarts (1½ liters) chicken or vegetable broth

1¼ cups (3dl) finely shaved Parmesan cheese

Salt and black pepper

FOR SERVING

3 tablespoons butter

25–30 sage leaves (fewer if, they are very large)

¾ cup (2dl) pumpkin seeds

Parmesan or Pecorino cheese, flaked or grated

Zest of 1 large lemon (preferably organic)

1. Peel and cut the pumpkin into ¾–1-inch (2–3cm) pieces. Peel and finely chop the onions and garlic. Add the olive oil to a large pot and sauté the onion and garlic until the onion is soft. Add the pumpkin, thyme, and rice and sauté for a couple of minutes until the rice gets a "shiny" look. Stir in the wine and let the mixture cook over medium heat. When the wine has reduced, add just enough warm broth so that the rice is covered. Bring to boil on low heat and then periodically add chicken broth gradually as the liquid boils down.

2. Melt the butter in a skillet over medium heat. Fry the sage leaves for 1–2 minutes until they start to get a little darker color. Turn the leaves during the cooking so that they fry evenly. Remove the crispy leaves and let them drain on paper towels. Roast the pumpkin seeds in the remaining butter in the skillet for a couple of minutes over medium heat until they get a light brown color. Stir the butter into the risotto. Let the rice simmer until it has become soft and the center still has a little firmness. Now stir vigorously and constantly until the rice is completely soft. Add more broth if needed. The risotto should be quite loose.

3. Once the rice is cooked al dente, stir in the Parmesan, season with salt and pepper, turn off the heat, and cover the pan. The cheese will bind everything together and the risotto will also thicken during the 5-minute period it needs to rest before serving.

4. Serve the risotto immediately with the Parmesan, sage leaves, pumpkin seeds, and lemon zest.

TWO-DAY BOLOGNESE

This Bolognese is not fast food—it need hours of cooking time to become as insanely good as it actually is. And it is worth every second on the stove! I usually make a big batch when it's time to clean the freezer, and the mix may include lamb, pork, different kinds of sausage, and stew meats. Any meat on the bone is especially good for this long-cooking Bolognese because it adds such deep flavor to the sauce. Oxtail in particular will give it a powerful *oompf*.

20 minutes + 3 ½ hours + at least 6 hours of rest time ▪ about 8 servings

2 yellow onions

4 cloves garlic

3 medium (300g) carrots

½ red chile, such as Fresno, seeded

4 large stalks celery

5 ounces (130g) salami or chorizo, salsiccia, or similar sausage

1 pound (500g) beef, such as prime rib, brisket, or rump steak

1 pound (500g) pork, such as loin or chops

3 tablespoons olive oil, or more, if needed

1¼ cups (3dl) red wine

3⅓ cups (8dl) water

2 14-ounce cans (800g) crushed tomatoes

2 tablespoons concentrated beef bouillon

2 tablespoons dried oregano

Salt and black pepper

1. Peel and finely chop the onions, garlic, and carrots. Finely chop the chile and celery. Slice the salami into thin pieces. Cut the beef and pork into small cubes.

2. Add the olive oil to a large saucepan and brown the beef, pork, and sausage. Transfer the meats and their juices to a separate saucepan. Check the first saucepan. If it's dry, add another tablespoon of olive oil and then place the onion, garlic, and chile into the saucepan and sauté until the onions are soft. Add the celery and carrots and sauté the mixture on high heat for a few minutes. Transfer the meats and their juices to the pot with the vegetable mix and add the wine, water, tomatoes, bouillon, and oregano. Season with salt and pepper.

3. Bring the mixture to a boil. Remove any scum that may have risen to the top of the pot, and continue to simmer the sauce over medium heat, partially covered, for about 2½ hours. Stir the sauce occasionally. Take the Bolognese off the heat and let it cool completely—preferably overnight. Then bring the Bolognese to a boil again, taste it and see if you need to season with more salt and pepper, and simmer for about 1 more hour. Serve with freshly boiled pasta and Pecorino or Parmesan cheese.

RISOTTO WITH BACON AND MUSHROOMS

Risotto is a wonderfully wholesome and soothing weekend dish. Here, it mingles with the earthy flavor of porcini mushrooms and smoky bacon. If you want to switch things up, replace the bacon with prosciutto—the end pieces that can't be cut into thin slices are particularly good in this risotto—just be sure to dice the meat finely.

45 minutes ▪ 4 servings

1 yellow onion

2 large cloves garlic

½ red chile, such as Fresno, seeded

10 ounces (300g) smoked, salted slab bacon, or prosciutto

7 ounces (200g) fresh mushrooms, porcini, chanterelles, or forest mushrooms

3 tablespoons olive oil

1¼ cups (3dl) carnaroli or Arborio rice

2 teaspoons dried rosemary

1¼ cups (3dl) unoaked, dry white wine

7 cups (16dl) chicken broth

1¼ cups (3dl) finely shaved Parmesan cheese, plus more for garnish

Salt and black pepper

1. Peel and slice the onion and garlic. Finely chop the chile. Finely dice the bacon (if you're using slab bacon, cut off the rind and outer fat on the bacon and finely dice the rest.) Clean the mushrooms and chop them into small pieces.

2. Add the olive oil to a large saucepan and sauté the onion, garlic, chile, bacon, and mushrooms until the onions are soft. Add the rice and rosemary and sauté for a few minutes while stirring. Pour in the wine and cook the mixture over low heat for a few minutes, stirring occasionally. Add enough broth to cover the rice and let it simmer over low heat, stirring occasionally. As the liquid boils off, gradually add the rest of the chicken broth. Let the rice simmer until it becomes soft and the center still has a little firmness. At that point, stir vigorously and constantly until the rice is completely soft. Add more broth if needed. The risotto should be quite loose.

2. Once the rice is cooked al dente, stir in the Parmesan, season with salt and pepper, turn of the heat, and cover the pan. The cheese will bind everything together and the risotto will also thicken during the 5-minute period it needs to rest before serving.

NOTE Dried mushrooms work equally well as fresh ones in this risotto, but you don't need to use as many of them. For example, if you choose to use dried porcini mushrooms, 1¾ ounces (50g, about 3 tablespoons) would be sufficient.

EGGS

Caprese Omelet with Pasta, 138

Plain Omelet, 140

Plain Scrambled Eggs, 141

Quick Fried Egg Sandwich with Avocado and
 Sriracha, 141

Scrambled Eggs with Good Things, 142

Mushrooms and Parsley, 142

Scrambled Eggs with Smoked Cream, 143

Smoked Salmon with Garden Cress and Lemon, 144

Poached Eggs with Ricotta and Nettles Sautéed
 In Butter, 145

Quiche with Chorizo, Tomatoes, and Beans, 146

Basic Pie Dough Recipe, 149

Scotch Eggs, 150

With eggs at home, there's always something to eat, and they're available year-round.

Eggs have a surprisingly long life. Properly stored in the refrigerator, fresh eggs can last at least two months. They make great road food when boiled and last up to one week in the fridge and more than a day at room temperature.

If you use only egg whites or egg yolks in a recipe, you can store the leftover portion of the eggs in an airtight jar in the refrigerator, where they'll keep for at least 4–5 days. With leftover egg whites you can make meringues and sorbets, among many other things, or simply fry the whites. A mix of egg whites and a generous tablespoon of cream is perfect for brushing on baked rolls and buns to ensure a burnished crust, and it makes an excellent glue for repairing cracks in a piecrust, after prebaking. Just brush the freshly baked piecrust with the egg white and cream mix, and let it rest in the oven for a couple of minutes to seal the cracks. Leftover egg yolks can be used in tiramisu, hollandaise, and Béarnaise sauce, chocolate frosting, baked goods, eggnog, protein drinks, and of course ice cream! The possibilities are endless.

CAPRESE OMELET
WITH
PASTA

If you're in the mood for a really robust omelet and just happen to have some chiles, garlic, and leftover cooked pasta (penne, fusilli, or farfalle, for example) lying around, you can enjoy a delicious mash-up that tastes more like a tortilla or a frittata than anything else, depending on what you use to fill the omelet. Give this one a try. I think you'll like it.

30 minutes ▪ 4 servings

8 eggs

½ cup (1¼ dl) liquid, such as cream, milk, or water

salt and black pepper

1 red onion

2 cloves garlic

½ red chile pepper, such as Fresno, seeded (optional)

½ zucchini

4 tablespoons olive oil

10 ounces (300g, about 1 pint) cherry tomatoes, chopped

1¼ cups (3dl) cooked pasta, such as penne, fusilli, or farfalle

7 ounces (200g) fresh mozzarella

Torn basil leaves, for serving

1. Whisk together the eggs and liquid, and season it with salt and pepper. Slice the onion and coarsely chop the garlic. Finely chop the chile pepper, if you're using it. Slice the zucchini very thin.

2. Heat the olive oil in a large frying pan and add the onions and tomatoes. Sauté the tomatoes until the skins begin to get a little wrinkled and gain some color. Stir in the garlic and, if using, the chile pepper, and sauté for a few minutes.

3. Reduce the heat and add the egg mixture to the pan and then the pasta. Add the zucchini and gently stir it into the egg-and-pasta mixture so that it is evenly distributed. Tear the mozzarella into pieces and sprinkle it over the top. Cook the omelet over low heat, stirring it gently now and then, until it starts to firm up. Continue to cook until the omelet has solidified but remains creamy in the middle.

4. Remove the pan from the heat, slide the omelet onto a plate, and garnish with a few fresh basil leaves. Serve the omelet with a good salad.

PLAIN OMELET

This is the kind of omelet that's great for breakfast or stuffed with various goodies for a quick lunch. To make a plain omelet, my formula is simple: 1 tablespoon of milk or other liquid, such as cream or water, and a little salt, per egg. Multiply based on your needs.

1. Quickly whisk together the eggs with the milk (or cream or water), and the salt. Don't overwork the egg mixture too much—it can be a little streaky. Add about 1 tablespoon of canola oil or butter to a frying pan over medium heat. Turn the pan so that the bottom of the pan is completely covered with the fat. Pour in the egg mixture and stir it with a fork. When the omelet begins to solidify, gently shake the pan a few times to gently loosen the edges.

2. When the bottom surface has solidified, but is the eggs are still a bit creamy, the omelet is done. This usually takes 5–8 minutes over medium heat (depending on whether you're frying a small or large omelet). To get the right consistency, don't fry the omelet over high heat. Rather, let it take a little longer to cook so that it stays creamy and delicate, without getting too brown or dry.

3. Loosen the omelet along the edges with a thin spatula and gently shake the pan so that the omelet comes loose. If the omelet doesn't come away from the pan, gently swipe the spatula underneath the omelet to release it. Lift the pan and tilt it away from you when you are sure that the omelet has loosened. When half of the omelet slides over the edge, use a large spatula to gently fold it over the other half in the pan.

4. To fill the omelet (see suggested fillings below), simply place the mixture over half the omelet. With a spatula, fold the other half of the omelet over the filling and gently slide the omelet onto a plate.

ALTERNATIVE FILLINGS

* Butter-fried mushrooms with parsley
* Grated, aged cheese, such as Cheddar
* Oven-baked tomatoes and mozzarella
* Meat sauce with lots of herbs
* Roasted bell peppers with spicy salami

PLAIN SCRAMBLED EGGS

There's nothing "plain" about scrambled eggs made with cream and good butter, but if you'd like something a little fancier and more robust, try some of the recipes starting on page 142.

5 minutes ▪ 4 servings

8 eggs

½ cup (1¼ dl) heavy cream

3 tablespoons butter

About ¼ teaspoon salt

1. In a bowl, stir together the eggs and cream with a fork.

2. Melt the butter with the salt in a saucepan over low heat. Pour in the egg and cream mixture and stir until the eggs start to firm up into creamy curds. Here' the secret to a creamy result: remove the eggs from the heat before they're completely done; they'll continue to cook and will be perfect when served.

QUICK FRIED EGG SANDWICH
with AVOCADO and SRIRACHA

The best thing about this open-faced sandwich is that the ingredients are almost always in the kitchen—and it can be made quickly. Sriracha is an addictively good chili sauce from Thailand, and a must-have in the pantry.

20 minutes ▪ 4 servings

4 slices light sourdough bread

2 heaping tablespoons butter, for frying the bread

4 eggs

Salt and freshly ground black pepper

2 ripe avocados

Sriracha sauce

½ cup (1 dl) roasted or caramelized onions

½ bunch fresh cilantro

1. Add 1 tablespoon of the butter to a pan and fry the bread slices until they're golden brown on both sides. Set them aside. Add the remaining tablespoon of butter to the pan and fry the eggs sunny side up, over medium heat, until the egg whites have coagulated, but the yolks are still a little runny. Season with salt and pepper.

2. Halve the avocados and removed their pits. Remove the peels and cut the avocado halves into slices. Layer the avocado evenly over the four slices of bread, top each with one egg, and then finish with Sriracha sauce, onions, and chopped cilantro. Serve immediately.

SCRAMBLED EGGS WITH GOOD THINGS

MUSHROOMS AND PARSLEY

15 minutes ■ **4 servings**

7 ounces (200g) oyster mushrooms
or other good mushrooms

2 tablespoons butter for frying
Salt and freshly ground black pepper

½ cup (1 dl) finely chopped parsley
Finely grated horseradish

1. Finely slice the mushrooms and fry them in the butter until they're golden brown. Season the mushrooms with salt and pepper and toss with the parsley.

2. Make the scrambled eggs using the basic recipe on page 141. Top the scrambled eggs with this mixture and serve immediately with a bit of the horseradish on top (you can also use a small dollop of prepared horseradish).

SCRAMBLED EGGS WITH SMOKED CREAM

15 minutes ▪ **4 servings**

½ cup (1 dl) heavy cream, smoked (see instructions below)

¾ cup (2dl) finely grated Pecorino or other good aged cheese

Freshly ground black pepper

1. To make the smoked cream: Pour the cream into a heatproof container. Cover the inside bottom of a pot with aluminum foil and put a few wood chips (milder fruit woods such as apple, cherry, and pear are particularly good) on top. Cover with foil. Put the lid on the pot, and set it over medium heat. When it starts to smoke heavily from the chips, insert the heatproof container. Cover the pot, take it off the heat, and set aside for 5 minutes. Now the smoked cream is ready!

2. To make the scrambled eggs: Use the basic recipe on page 141 and replace the heavy cream with Smoked Cream. Top the eggs with Pecorino and freshly ground black pepper.

> **NOTE**   Make sure your kitchen is well ventilated before you start smoking the cream. You don't want your smoke alarm to go off. Make sure that your kitchen smoke alarm is installed at least 10 feet (3m) from your cooking appliances. It should be mounted high on the wall or ceiling (smoke rises), and installed not more than 12 inches (30cm) away from the ceiling.

SMOKED SALMON WITH GARDEN CRESS AND LEMON

15 minutes ▪ **4 servings**

4 slices smoked salmon

    Freshly ground black pepper

1 cup loosely packed fresh garden cress

    Grated zest of 1 lemon

1. Shred the salmon and place it on warm, scrambled eggs, using the basic recipe on page 141. Season with freshly ground pepper and garnish with garden cress and lemon zest.

POACHED EGGS with RICOTTA AND NETTLES SAUTÉED in BUTTER

Poached eggs are some of the tastiest things I know and are mighty impressive.

25 minutes ■ 4 servings

3 (ounces) (100g) tender nettles, kale, or baby spinach

2 tablespoons butter for frying

1 large clove garlic

Salt and black pepper

4 fresh quail eggs, preferably, but chicken eggs work well

4 slices of good bread, preferably a light sourdough

¾ cup (2dl) ricotta cheese

2 tablespoons (25g) aged cheese, such as a sharp Cheddar

Pecorino or Parmesan cheese

Grated lemon peel

1. Fill a pot with water and bring it to a boil. Immerse the nettles in the boiling water for 30 seconds. Remove them from the pot and drain them on paper towels. Remove the tender nettle leaves from the stems, reserving the leaves only. (If you are using kale or spinach as a substitute for the nettles: drain the steamed leaves and go to Step 2.)

2. Put the butter in a frying pan and sauté the leaves for a few minutes. Finely chop the garlic and sauté it in the pan with the nettles at the last minute. Season with salt and pepper and set aside.

3. To poach the eggs, bring 1 quart water, 1 tablespoon vinegar, and 1 teaspoon salt to a boil. Prepare a bowl with about 1½ cups water and 2 tablespoons vinegar. Crack 4 fresh eggs into the bowl of water. Let stand for about 2 minutes and then slowly pour everything into the boiling water. Simmer for about 4 minutes. Shake the pot gently if the eggs sink to the bottom so they won´t stick. Remove the eggs one at a time with a slotted spoon.

4. Toast the bread and then fry it in butter, if you like. Top each slice with some of the ricotta, nettles, and finally a poached egg. Finish with a sprinkle of cheese and lemon zest and serve immediately.

QUICHE WITH CHORIZO, TOMATOES, AND BEANS

Is there anything better than a really good quiche? This one is loaded with especially good things—spicy chorizo, creamy white beans, and the bright acid tang of cherry tomatoes. Serve it with a green salad and a good glass of wine.

30 minutes + 30 minutes in the fridge + about 75 minutes in the oven ■ 4–6 servings

PASTRY
See the basic recipe on page 149.

FILLING

1 large leek, pale part of the bulb (save the rest for a different dish)

1 large clove garlic

10 small cherry tomatoes

1 14-ounce can (400g) white beans

1½ dried chorizo, skin removed

½ cup (1 dl) oregano leaves picked off the stems

6 eggs

2 cups (5dl) half-and-half

Salt and freshly ground black pepper

1 package (5 ounces; 150g) feta cheese (either sheep or goat's milk)

1. Preheat the oven to 400°F (200°C).

2. To make the pastry, follow the instructions for basic pie dough on page 149. Prebake the pie dough in a 9-inch (23cm) springform pan.

3. Remove the aluminum foil covering the outer edge of the crust after prebaking.

4. Slice leek and carefully rinse it in cold water to remove any sand or grit. Chop the garlic and halve the cherry tomatoes. Rinse and drain the white beans. Cut the chorizo into small cubes and chop the oregano finely. Layer all the ingredients into the prebaked piecrust.

5. Mix the eggs, half-and-half, and butter, and season with salt and pepper. Pour the mixture over the ingredients in the piecrust. Give the pie a gentle jiggle to make sure that the egg mixture is evenly distributed (and not pooling on top of the filling). Crumble the feta cheese over the top.

6. Reduce the oven heat to 350°F (175°C) and bake the pie on the bottom rack the oven for about 1 hour, or until the egg mixture has solidified and the pie starts to turn golden brown. Let the quiche rest for about 20 minutes before serving.

BASIC PIE DOUGH RECIPE

This pie dough recipe is simple—and perfect. It works every time. Use it to make Quiche with Chorizo, Tomatoes, and Beans (on page 146) and for all your pie baking.

10 minutes + 30 minutes in refrigerator ▪ **4–6 portions**

7 tablespoons (100g) cold butter

2 cups (4½ dl) flour

½ cup (4 ounces, 100g) quark or ricotta cheese

½ teaspoon salt

1. Cut the butter into cubes. Working quickly with a food processor or by hand, combine the butter with the flour, quark or ricotta, and salt to form a dough.

2. Knead the dough a little on lightly floured surface. Roll it out into a ⅛-in (3mm) thick circle. Gently press the dough into a springform pan or a pie pan. Trim the dough hanging over the side of the pan to about 1 inch (2cm). Fold it under itself to form a rim, and then pinch the dough together with your fingers. Cover the dough in the pan with plastic wrap and refrigerate for 30 minutes.

3. Meanwhile, preheat the oven to 450°F (225°C). Remove the plastic wrap from the pie pan and prick the bottom crust with a fork. Cover the edges of the piecrust with aluminum foil and prebake it in the oven for about 12 minutes or until the crust is a light golden brown.

SCOTCH EGGS

I had Scotch Eggs for the first time in a pub in London and, as a sausage, fried-food, and egg lover, I fell head over heels—three good things at the same time! This recipe might seem a little finicky, but it's definitely worth the effort.

40 minutes ▪ 4 servings

6 eggs

1 pound (500g) fresh, raw chorizo (not dried)

⅔ cup (1½ dl) finely chopped chives

About 1 quart (1 liter) of cooking oil

1–2 cups (2–3 dl) panko (Japanese bread crumbs)

Sea salt (Maldon, if you have any on hand)

1. Bring a pot of water to a boil. Boil 4 eggs in the water for 2 minutes. Remove the eggs, let them rest on a plate for 2 minutes, and then rinse them in cold water until they are completely cold. Peel them very carefully.

2. Remove the skin from the sausages and shape the sausage meat into four balls. Roll out each ball, between plastic wrap, into 4 thin circles large enough large to cover an egg.

3. Sprinkle the chives onto the rounds. Add an egg to the middle of each circle and cover it completely with the sausage and chive mixture. Work carefully so that the eggs don't break.

4. Wrap the eggs in plastic wrap and refrigerate them while you heat a deep pot of frying oil to around 325°F (160 °C). Check the temperature with a cooking thermometer. You'll know the oil is hot enough if you toss a small piece of white bread into the oil and it turns golden brown after about 1 minute.

5. Beat the remaining two eggs in a bowl. Pour the panko in another bowl. Remove the plastic wrap from the egg balls. Dip them in the beaten egg and then roll them in the panko crumbs so that they are fully covered. Fry the egg balls in the oil for 7–9 minutes or until they're golden brown and the sausage mixture is thoroughly cooked. Remove the eggs from the oil with a slotted spoon and drain them on paper towels. Sprinkle the Scotch Eggs with sea salt and serve them immediately, preferably with good-quality mayonnaise or chili sauce. If you want to go the traditional route, serve the Scotch Eggs with a wedge of excellent, aged Cheddar cheese, pickles, and pickled onions.

DESSERTS AND OTHER BAKED GOODS

This is the season for richer, gooier, fudgier, and sweeter desserts, if you ask me—the finger-licking-good ending to a dinner. Here you'll find warmer, heartier sweets that include chocolate, nuts, and rich glistening creams to help soothe your soul when cold winter weather sets in. Whether it's a humble fruit crumble or a fancy-but-easy-to-make Tiramisu Trifle, you'll find something to love and share with your family.

If you're entertaining guests or just want to make the splendid desserts in this chapter look extra special, serve them in a pretty glass jar or bowl or on your grandma's best china. It'll make everyone feel extra special.

In this chapter, you'll also find a recipe for quick muffins and one for fruity rye bread, for those times when you want something sweet but not too sweet or dessert-like. You'll enjoy the muffins and bread. Try them for breakfast, with some nice cheese or a late afternoon snack with a cup of hot coffee or tea.

APPLE CARAMEL PIE
WITH
ALMOND CRUMBLE

My approach to desserts is "the more, the merrier." I'll gladly take extra of everything when it comes to nuts, caramel, fruit, chocolate, and meringues. So this particular pie is high on my list of favorites. How can you go wrong with caramel, tart apples, and a deliciously sweet and salty, crunchy almond crumble? Peel the apples if you like; if I'm in a hurry I leave the peel on, and the pie tastes just as good.

About 25 minutes + about 35 minutes oven time ▪ 4–6 servings

6 tart apples

¾ cup (2dl) granulated sugar

¾ cup (2dl) golden syrup or light corn syrup

1½ cups (4dl) heavy cream

CRUMBLE TOPPING

5 ounces (150g, 1 cup) almonds

1 cup (225g) butter, chilled and cubed

3 tablespoons (½dl) brown sugar

1¼ cups (3dl) flour

1 teaspoon salt

1 egg

FOR SERVING

Soft whipped cream or cream mixed with full-fat Greek yogurt

1. Preheat the oven to 350°F (175°C). Core and cut the apples into wedges.

2. Pour the sugar, syrup, and cream into a large ovenproof frying pan with high sides and let the sugar melt over low heat. Don't stir the mixture while the sugar is melting or you will get lumps in it. Add the apple wedges and toss so that the caramel covers them thoroughly.

3. Finely chop the almonds for the crumble topping in a food processor. Add the butter, brown sugar, flour, salt, and egg to the food processor and mix to form a crumbly dough. Spread the dough over the apple wedges in the ovenproof frying pan, and set the pan in the middle of the oven. Bake for 30–35 minutes or until the crumble has turned a fine golden color.

4. Serve the pie with soft whipped cream or a mixture of cream mixed with full-fat Greek yogurt.

TIRAMISU TRIFLE

A classic tiramisu needs at least 10 hours in the refrigerator to be truly worthy, but sometimes the urge to have this decadent treat takes over with such furious momentum that you have to have it sooner. When that happens, try this variation. It only takes a couple of hours in the fridge to reach perfection, but if you do have more time, prepare it a day in advance—it only gets better.

15 minutes + 2 hours ▪ 4 servings

8 ounces (250g, 1 cup) mascarpone

½ cup (1 dl) powdered sugar

1 tablespoon cocoa

3 tablespoons Baileys Irish Cream

¾ cup (2dl) + 2 tablespoons whipping cream, divided

12 ladyfinger cookies

⅔ cup (1½dl) cold strong coffee

1. Whisk together the mascarpone, powdered sugar, cocoa, Baileys, and 2 tablespoons of the cream in a bowl. In another bowl, whisk the remaining ¾ cup (2dl) whipping cream until fluffy.

2. Layer the cream and mascarpone into 4 glasses. Dip the cookies quickly, one at a time, in the coffee and then immediately insert them into the glasses so that there are 3 cookies in each glass. Refrigerate for at least 2 hours before serving.

APPLE CRUMBLE PIE MILKSHAKE

What is it that people really like about apple crumble pie? Is it the sweet mix of sugar and oats on top? The tartness from the apples? The spicy cinnamon? Or is it the scoop of vanilla ice cream on top of the crumble that makes it so delicious? Here you get all those fabulous flavors faster than you can say "crumble." Just remember to take the ice cream out of the freezer in advance so that it's not too hard to mix into the shake.

5 minutes ■ 4 servings

2 apples

8 oatmeal cookies, crumbled

1¾ cups (4dl) cold milk

2 teaspoons ground cinnamon plus additional for garnish

1 quart (8dl) vanilla ice cream

1. Peel, core, and cut the apples into thick pieces. Put the pieces in a blender together with the crumbled cookies. Blend until the mixture has a smooth consistency. Add the milk, cinnamon, and ice cream and blend until smooth and a bit fluffy.
2. Pour the milkshake into 4 sundae glasses, dust the tops with a little cinnamon, and serve immediately.

NOTE If you want a slightly more grown-up and luxurious taste, add a little splash of Calvados. It's dangerously good!

POACHED APPLES IN COINTREAU AND SAFFRON SYRUP

Poached pears are a classic, but why is the method so rarely used when it comes to apples? In this recipe, I use small apples, but if you don't have them, just split large ones in half and cook them in a little less time. Apples can get a little mushier than pears when they're cooked, so keep an eye on them. You want them to keep their shape in the Cointreau and saffron syrup.

30 minutes ▪ 4 servings

5–6 small apples

1¾ cups (4dl) water

¾ cup (2dl) sugar

⅔ cup (1½dl) Cointreau

1 teaspoon coarsely ground cardamom

1 teaspoon saffron threads

FOR SERVING

Vanilla ice cream or lightly whipped cream

1. Peel and core the apples. Bring the water, sugar, Cointreau, cardamom, and saffron to a boil in large, wide saucepan to make the syrup. Then place the apples, cut side down, into the hot syrup. Simmer the apples gently in the saucepan, covered, for about 10 minutes. Gently turn the apples and simmer them in the pan for another 10 minutes. Take the pan off the heat and let the apples cool in the syrup. When the apples are completely cool, store them in clean jar with a tight-fitting lid.

2. Serve the apples with vanilla ice cream or whipped cream. The apples can stay in the refrigerator for 1–2 months covered in the syrup.

CRISPY PEAR COBBLER

The sweetness of the toffee in the crumble crust does a magnificent job of balancing any tartness in the pears and also gives this cobbler a delightfully crispy shell. If you like, you can use tart apples instead of pears—it's just as delicious!

45 minutes ■ 4 servings

4 soft pears, preferably Anjou or another slightly acidic variety

Peel and juice from ½ orange (preferably organic)

Juice of ½ lemon

10 tablespoons (150g) butter

¼ cup (½dl) heavy cream

¼ cup (½dl) corn syrup

¾ cup (2dl) rolled oats

¾ cup (2dl) flour

1 teaspoon baking soda

2 pinches of salt

¾ cup (2dl) sugar

1. Preheat the oven to 350°F (175°C). Peel, core, and slice the pears very thinly. Put them in a large bowl with the orange peel, orange juice, and lemon juice. Set aside.

2. Melt the butter in a cast iron or other ovenproof pan, about 9 inches (23cm) in diameter, with high sides. Add the cream and corn syrup and stir. Add the oats, flour, baking soda, salt, and sugar. Stir to combine. Gently press the pear slices into the mixture in the pan. Set the pan on the middle rack in the oven and bake for about 25 minutes or until the top has turned golden brown and the sides are nicely caramelized.

BAKED APPLE
AND
CINNAMON BUN PUDDING

This hearty wintertime dessert is a delectable mash-up of two of my favorite things—cinnamon buns and pudding—and it includes apples, too, another favorite. I think of it as the ultimate Sunday dessert and a great way to use up any leftover cinnamon buns (as unlikely as that may sound). This dessert is a real treat.

50 minutes ■ 4–6 servings

¼ cup (½dl) sugar

¾ cup (2dl) heavy cream

3 eggs

1 tablespoon cinnamon

8 day-old cinnamon buns

2 large apples

CINNAMON SYRUP

3 cinnamon sticks

½ cup (1 dl) brown sugar

⅔ cup (1½dl) water

FOR SERVING

Whipped cream

Cinnamon syrup (optional)

1. Preheat the oven to 400°F (200°C). Gently stir together the sugar, cream, eggs, and cinnamon in a bowl. Break the cinnamon buns into small pieces and fold them into the cream mixture. Let it rest for 25 minutes. Meanwhile, core the apples and cut them into thin slices. Gently mix the apple slices with the mixture in the bowl.

2. Pour the mixture into a 9-inch (23cm) pie pan or gratin dish. Use a spatula to get all the liquid from the bowl into the pan. Bake the pudding on the middle rack of the oven for 20–25 minutes.

3. While the pudding is baking, put the cinnamon sticks, brown sugar, and water in a small saucepan and bring to a boil. Simmer the mixture until it thickens and becomes syrupy, about 5 minutes.

4. Serve the pudding warm with the cinnamon syrup and a dollop of whipped cream on top. Of course the pudding will taste just as good without the syrup, if you want a less sweet dessert.

CHOCOLATE RISOTTO
WITH
RASPBERRIES

Risotto for dessert? Absolutely! Dark chocolate makes this risotto fit for a party. The addition of fresh or half-thawed raspberries cuts through the rich creaminess of this dessert to give it a fresh, acid bite. This one's a keeper.

30 minutes ▪ 4–6 servings

2 tablespoons butter

¾ cup (2dl) carnaroli or Arborio rice

2 cups (5dl) water

½ teaspoon salt

3 cups (7dl) milk

7 ounces (200g) 55% dark chocolate

7 ounces (200g, about 2 cups) semi-thawed or fresh raspberries

Flaked salt

1. Melt the butter in a large saucepan. Add the rice to the pan and sauté, stirring for about 1 minute. Pour in the water, add the salt, and bring to a boil. Simmer the rice uncovered until the water has been absorbed. Stir frequently. (This makes the risotto creamy.) Add the milk and reduce the heat slightly. Continue to simmer while stirring, until the rice is tender and most of the liquid has been absorbed. Add more milk if needed. Take the pan off the heat.

2. Chop the chocolate and add it to the mixture into the saucepan. Stir thoroughly until the chocolate has melted. Serve the risotto immediately with the raspberries and a scattering of flaked salt on top. Keep in mind that risotto solidifies when it cools. To reheat it, add a dash of milk and warm over very low heat.

> **NOTE** If you want a sweeter risotto, try exchanging ¼ cup of the milk with sweetened condensed milk. Add it at the same time you stir in the chocolate.

NUTELLA AND BANANA "PIES"

You don't always have to be so hard on yourself, especially when you're making dessert. It should be fun! And what could be easier than making mini puff pastries in a muffin pan? The filling— Nutella and banana slices—couldn't be easier to make. If don't have a muffin pan, you can bake these delightful treats in small ramekins or soufflé dishes. Whatever pan you use, don't forget to grease it with a little butter.

About 40 minutes ▪ 4 servings

4 squares (about 5 × 5 inches; 14 × 14cm) puff pastry

2 ripe bananas

⅔ cup (1½dl) Nutella

1 pinch flaked salt

½ teaspoon sugar

½ teaspoon ground cinnamon

5 teaspoons melted butter

FOR SERVING
Vanilla ice cream or soft whipped cream

1. Preheat the oven to 400°F (200°C). Grease four compartments in a muffin pan (or four small ramekins or soufflé dishes), with butter and gently press a square of puff pastry into each form. The puff pastry should be a little loose and hang over the sides about ⅓–½ inch (1–2cm).

2. Peel and slice the bananas. Layer the banana and Nutella in the puff pastry molds and top them with the flaked salt. In a small bowl, mix the sugar and cinnamon. Brush the puff pastry that is hanging over the sides of the molds with melted butter and sprinkle it with the sugar mixture. Gently fold the sides toward the middle of the molds.

3. Bake the pastries on the middle rack of the oven for about 25 minutes or until they've turned golden brown. Let them cool for about 10 minutes and then serve the little "pies" with a scoop of vanilla ice cream or a dollop of soft whipped cream.

CHOCOLATE SAUCE
WITH
PORTER

Here you have a superb chocolate sauce that adds a touch of sophistication to both everyday ice cream cones and festive sundaes, as well as the bowl of ice cream you want to enjoy for absolutely no reason at all. Make a double batch, while you're at it. I promise, you'll use all of this sauce.

5 minutes ▪ 4 servings

5 ounces (150g) 70% dark chocolate

½ cup (1 dl) porter (beer)

½ cup (1 dl) heavy cream

½ teaspoon salt

2 tablespoons butter

FOR SERVING

Chocolate ice cream

Brownie pieces

Flaked salt (optional)

1. Finely chop the chocolate. In a small saucepan, bring the porter and heavy cream to a boil. Remove the saucepan from the heat and stir in the chocolate. Continue to stir until the chocolate has completely melted. Add the salt and butter and stir until the butter has melted. Let the sauce cool.

2. Scoop some chocolate ice cream into the bowls, sprinkle with brownie pieces, and drizzle the top of each serving with a generous amount of the chocolate sauce. If you like, sprinkle some flaked salt on top and serve.

ALMOND CREAM WITH APPLE COMPOTE

This delicious, smooth, almond-flavored dessert is as light as a cream puff. It's the perfect dessert to make a day ahead of time if you're expecting guests or just want to surprise your family with something special.

About 30 minutes + 2 hours in the fridge ▪ 4 servings

1 vanilla pod
4 ounces (125g) almond paste
1⅓ cups (3¼dl) milk
½ cup (1 dl) powdered sugar
1 packet (7g) unflavored gelatin powder
1 cup (2½dl) heavy cream

APPLE COMPOTE

4 small apples
½ cup (1 dl) sugar
2 teaspoons freshly ground cardamom
Toasted slivered almonds for garnish

1. Slice the vanilla pod lengthwise and scrape out the seeds. In a medium saucepan, mix the almond paste with the milk, powdered sugar, and vanilla seeds. Bring the mixture to a boil and let it simmer for a few minutes while stirring. Take the pan off the heat and let the mixture cool slightly.

2. Pass the mixture through a fine sieve into a medium bowl. Sprinkle the gelatin over the warm liquid in the bowl, and let it rest for 3–5 minutes. Whisk until the gelatin has dissolved. Place the bowl in a cold-water bath (see Note), and stir until the mixture has cooled.

3. In a separate bowl, whip the cream until it is fluffy, and then fold it into the cooled almond/milk mixture. Gently mix until everything has come together. Spoon the creamy mixture into a few pretty glasses or small jars, cover them with plastic wrap, and refrigerate for at least 2 hours.

4. Core and peel the apples. Cut them into small cubes and mix them with the sugar and cardamom in a medium bowl. Transfer the apples to a small saucepan, and stir them over high heat until they start to break down. Add a little water if the apples are not releasing enough liquid, and continue to stir over low heat until the apples cook down into a rough compote. Add a little more water, if needed.

5. Garnish the little glasses or jars of almond cream with the apple compote and finish with a sprinkling of toasted almonds.

> **NOTE** To prepare a cold-water bath, fill a large metal bowl with ice water and ice cubes. Make sure the bowl is big enough to accommodate the size of the saucepan or mixing bowl that will rest in the cold-water bath.

APPLE NOUGAT FRITTERS

Washed down with a glass of cold milk, these fritters, filled with nougat and applesauce, and then rolled in cinnamon and sugar, are just about the tastiest things you can stuff yourself with.

45 minutes + 1½ hours rising time ▪ About 24 fritters

½ cup (1 dl) lukewarm milk

3 tablespoons (25g) crumbled fresh yeast

2¾ cups (6½dl) flour, divided, plus additional for rolling out dough

6 tablespoons (75g) softened butter

¼ cup (½dl) sugar, divided

2 eggs

3 ounces (100g) nougat candy

½ cup (1 dl) applesauce

About 1 quart (about 1 liter) cooking oil

About 2 tablespoons cinnamon

About 3 tablespoons sugar, for coating the fritters

1. In a small saucepan, heat the milk to 98°F (37°C). Crumble the yeast into a bowl and stir the warm milk into the yeast. Mix ¾ cups (2dl) of the flour into the bowl and let it rise, covered, for about 20 minutes.

2. In a separate bowl, beat the butter and ¼ cup of the sugar until smooth. Mix in the eggs, one at a time, and don't worry if the batter looks like it's separating. Stir the butter mixture into the bowl containing the risen batter. Then stir in the rest of the flour and quickly work it into a firm dough.

3. Scrape the dough onto a generously floured surface. Roll out the dough until it is about ¼ inch (½cm) thick. Using a small juice glass or cookie cutter, 3–4 inches (8–10cm) in diameter, punch out about 24 circles. Add a walnut-size ball of nougat to the middle of each circle, along with ½–1 teaspoon of applesauce. Pinch the edges together at the top and form it into a ball. Set each fritter seam-side

down on a plate or cookie sheet lined with parchment paper. Cover with a clean kitchen towel and let the dough rise for about 1 hour.

4. Heat the oil in a large saucepan until it reaches 335–350°F (170–180°C). (If you have an exhaust fan, be sure it is turned off. Keep the saucepan lid close by. If the oil catches fire, cover the saucepan and turn off the heat.) Use a kitchen thermometer to control the temperature. To test the temperature, drop a small piece of white bread into the oil. If it turns golden brown in about 30 seconds the temperature is right.

5. Fry 3–4 fritters at a time until they turn golden brown, 3 minutes. Turn them over about halfway through. Remove the fritters from the hot oil using a slotted spoon and let them drain on a wire rack. Meanwhile, in a large bowl, mix the remaining sugar and the cinnamon together, and toss the fritters in the mix to coat them while still warm.

NOTE These fritters taste best of all freshly fried and even a bit lukewarm, but they're fine to freeze as well. But don't roll them in cinnamon sugar until just before serving them. After defrosting them, spritz with a little water and reheat them gently in oven or microwave. That way, when you roll them in the cinnamon sugar mixture, they'll get coated as easily as when they were just fried.

BROWNIES WITH THE WORLD'S BEST CHOCOLATE FROSTING

This super rich, triple-chocolate brownie is the perfect dessert. The chocolate frosting, studded with salted peanuts and almonds, makes it extra decadent. You can also use the recipe for the brownie in another super rich dessert—Eton Mess with Brownie and Caramel Sauce (page 180).

About 45 minutes ■ About 20 brownies

CHOCOLATE FROSTING

7 ounces (200g) 70% dark chocolate

½ cup (1 dl) heavy cream

¼ cup (½dl) honey

4 teaspoons softened butter

BROWNIE

1 cup (225g) butter

11 ounces (300g) 70% dark chocolate

4 eggs

1¾ cups (250g) dark muscovado or dark brown sugar

1 teaspoon salt

1 heaping cup (165g) all-purpose flour

½ cup (1 dl) cocoa

1 cup (150g) peanuts and almonds

TOPPING

¾ cup (100g) salted peanuts

¾ cup (100g) almonds

1. For the frosting, finely chop the chocolate and put it in a bowl. In a small saucepan, bring the cream and honey to a boil and pour the hot mixture over the chocolate. Stir until the chocolate has melted. Allow the chocolate to cool to about 100°F (38°C), using a candy thermometer to check the temperature. Stir the frosting to make it cool faster. Cut the butter into small cubes and add it in batches to the chocolate mixture, beating vigorously. When the frosting is smooth and shiny, set it aside.

2. Preheat the oven to 350°F (175°C). To make the brownie, melt the butter in a heavy saucepan. Meanwhile, coarsely chop 7 ounces (200g) of the dark chocolate and stir it into the saucepan. Remove the pan from the heat, and stir the chocolate into the butter until it has melted. Let the mixture cool slightly. In a bowl, stir together (don't whisk) the eggs and sugar. Add the chocolate and butter mixture to the eggs and sugar, and add the salt. Stir to combine. Mix the flour and cocoa together in a separate bowl and sift them into the brownie batter. Fold the flour and cocoa mixture into the brownie batter with a spatula. Finely chop the remaining 4 ounces (100g) of dark chocolate, and roughly chop the peanuts and almonds. Fold them into the batter.

3. Line an 8 × 12-inch (20 × 30cm) baking pan with parchment paper, and pour the batter into the pan. Bake the brownie on the middle rack of the oven for about 35 minutes. When you remove it from the oven, it should still be a little moist in the middle (and it will continue to cook in the pan). It is always better to underbake brownies a little bit in order to keep them moist. Let the brownie cool completely in the pan (overnight if possible, to keep them chewy).

4. Spread the chocolate frosting over the brownie. Coarsely chop the peanuts and almonds and sprinkle them over the top. Cut the brownie into squares. Refrigerate them for about 15 minutes before serving. Extra brownies (if there are any, that is) can be frozen for a few days. Thaw them slowly at room temperature.

ETON MESS WITH BROWNIE AND CARAMEL SAUCE

I'm breaking all the rules here and replacing the broken meringue in Eton mess, a British favorite—and a classic, old-school dessert—with a brownie from the recipe on page 179. And of course the caramel sauce in my variation, with its shot of bourbon or dark rum, is a departure from the summery innocence of the original formula. I've used raspberries instead of strawberries as well, but feel free to use any fresh berries you can find (even thawed frozen fruit will work)—and be generous with the cream. This is a colorful, festive dessert, so reserve it for a particularly gloomy winter's day and share it with your family and friends. It will cheer everyone up!

About 30 minutes ▪ 4 servings

4 ounces (100g) milk chocolate

1 cup + 2 tablespoons (250g) butter

1¼ cups (250g) light or dark muscovado sugar or light or dark brown sugar

1 cup (2½dl) heavy cream

5 tablespoons bourbon or dark rum

Flaked salt to taste

¾ cup (2dl) heavy cream

4 pieces of brownie (from the recipe for Brownies with the World's Best Chocolate Frosting on page 179)

⅔ cup (1½dl) roasted nuts of your choice

1¼ cups (3dl) fresh raspberries (or frozen and thawed berries of your choice)

1. To make the caramel sauce, roughly chop the chocolate, cut the butter into pieces, and put them into a heavy saucepan with the muscovado (or brown) sugar. Gently heat the mixture over low heat until the chocolate and sugar have melted. Stir occasionally. Remove the saucepan from the heat and whisk in the cream, bourbon, and salt flakes. Let the sauce cool in the refrigerator.

2. Whip the cream until fluffy. Break the brownie in bite-size pieces and coarsely chop the roasted nuts.

3. Layer brownie pieces, cream, caramel sauce, nuts, and raspberries in bowls or on plates and serve immediately—or layer in pretty glasses and refrigerate for a few hours before serving.

NOTE Leftover caramel sauce keeps for a couple of weeks in the refrigerator. It can crystallize a little, but warming it up will correct that.

RICH MARBLE CAKE

Swirls of chocolate and vanilla (the best of both worlds) make this delightful, easy dessert pretty enough for company, but it also makes a great afternoon snack with a cup of coffee or tea. Your kids won't mind it a bit they find a generous slice in their lunch box.

About 20 minutes + about 1 hour in the oven ▪ 12 servings

CHOCOLATE BATTER

¼ cup (60dl) milk

5 tablespoons (75g) butter

¼ cup (25dl) cocoa powder

2 pinches of salt

1 egg

½ cup (1 dl) sugar

½ cup (1 dl) flour

1 teaspoon baking powder

4 ounces (100g) dark chocolate, chopped

VANILLA BATTER

3 eggs

⅔ cup (1½dl) granulated sugar

⅔ cup (1½dl) half-and-half

7 tablespoons (100g) butter

1¾ cups (4dl) all-purpose flour

¾ cup (2dl) almond flour

1 tablespoon vanilla sugar

2 teaspoons baking powder

FOR ASSEMBLY

⅔ cup (1½dl) coarsely chopped nuts, such as walnuts, pecans, or hazelnuts

1. Preheat the oven to 350°F (175°C). Grease and flour a 7½ × 3-inch (6 cup; 19 × 8cm) Bundt pan.

2. To make the chocolate batter: Bring the milk to a boil in a heavy saucepan. Add the butter and let it melt on low hear, then whisk in the cocoa and salt and let the mixture simmer for a minute, as you stir it. In a bowl, whisk the egg and sugar until fluffy. In a separate bowl, mix the flour and baking powder. Whisk the butter mixture into the egg mixture. Then fold in the dry ingredients and chocolate pieces.

3. To make the vanilla batter: Whisk the eggs and sugar until fluffy in a bowl. Bring the half-and-half to a boil in a heavy saucepan and remove it from the heat. Add the butter. When the butter has melted, stir in the egg and sugar mixture. In another bowl, mix the all-purpose and almond flours, vanilla sugar, and baking powder, and then fold them into the wet ingredients to make a smooth batter.

4. Layer the vanilla batter and chocolate batter and nuts in the pan. To create marbling, run a fork or a table knife through the batters in a swirling motion. Bake the cake on the bottom rack of the oven, rotating the pan halfway through, for 50–60 minutes or until a toothpick comes out clean. Transfer the cake to a rack to cool for a few minutes, and then turn it out of the pan and let it cool completely on the rack.

BANANA-TOFFEE CAKE

The interplay of tangy yogurt, sweet ripe bananas, and the rich caramel flavor of toffee make this banana cake extra tasty and moist. It gets even better after a day or two and can be sliced, toasted, and buttered for a decadent breakfast treat.

About 20 minutes + about 1 hour in the oven ▪ **12 servings**

¾ cup (175g) softened butter

¾ cup (2dl) sugar

3 eggs, room temperature

3 large, very ripe bananas

1¼ cups (3dl) plain yogurt

2 tablespoons cold, strong coffee

2½ cups (6dl) all-purpose flour

½ cup (1 dl) cocoa powder

1 tablespoon vanilla sugar

1 tablespoon baking powder

½ teaspoon salt

4 ounces (113g) chocolate toffee, broken into small pieces

1. Preheat the oven to 350°F (175°C). Grease and flour a 9 × 5-inch (23 × 13cm) loaf pan.

2. In a bowl, beat the butter and sugar with a whisk until it is fluffy. Add one egg at a time to the bowl, continuing to whisk (don't worry if the mixture breaks). In a separate bowl, mash the bananas. Add the yogurt and coffee to the mashed bananas. Stir the egg mixture into the banana mixture.

3. In another bowl, mix the flour, cocoa powder, vanilla sugar, baking powder, and salt. Stir the banana mixture into the dry ingredients. Stir together to form a smooth batter and pour it into the loaf pan. Scatter the broken pieces of toffee on top of the batter.

4. Bake the banana bread on the lower rack of the oven for 60–70 minutes or until a toothpick comes out clean. Let the pan cool on a rack for about 20 minutes, and then turn it out of the pan and let it cool completely on the rack.

FRUITY DARK RYE BREAD

This is a great bread to have in winter, because it is rich and heavy with raisins and seeds (or nuts, if you prefer). It makes a hearty snack with a cup of strong, hot coffee or tea and is delicious for breakfast—just slice the bread, toast it, and spread it with some good butter, cream cheese, or even a soft brie or goat cheese, if you like sweet-salty combos. Feel free to replace the raisins with dried apricots, figs, tart cherries, or prunes, and the seeds with chopped walnuts or pistachios, slice almonds, or any other nuts you might like. This is an easy bread to make, too, because there's no yeast, no kneading, and no rising time—but it's a dense bread and has a long baking time. The wait is well worth it!

about 20 minutes + 75 minutes in the oven ▪ 2 loaves

4 ounces (125g) cracked wheat

4 ounces (125g) cracked rye

½ cup (1 dl) raisins

½ cup (1 dl) flaxseed

¼ cup (½dl) sunflower seeds

1 tablespoon baking soda

2 teaspoons salt

2 tablespoons wheat bran

5¼ cups (12½dl) all-purpose flour

1 quart (1 liter) buttermilk

½ cup (1 dl) dark corn syrup

Oatmeal for sprinkling over the top of the bread (optional)

1. Preheat the oven to 300°F (150°C). In a large bowl, mix together the wheat, rye, raisins, flaxseed, sunflower seeds, baking soda, salt, wheat bran, and flour. Add the buttermilk and syrup, and stir to combine into a batter. Grease two 8½ × 4-inch (21 × 11 cm) bread loaf pans and distribute the batter evenly in the two pans. Sprinkle the tops with oatmeal, if you like.

2. Bake the loaves on the middle rack of the oven for about 75 minutes. The bread is done when it comes away from the sides of the pan. Turn the loaves out of the pans as soon as they come out of the oven and let them cool on a wire rack, lightly covered with a clean dishtowel.

QUICK MUFFINS WITH CARDAMOM, APPLE, AND NUTS

These quick muffins bake super fast and are easy to vary with an almost endless list of nuts, spices, berries, and other fruit. They're great for breakfast or a late-afternoon snack, when you want something sweet—but not too sweet. These will definitely hit the spot.

About 25 minutes + 25 minutes in the oven ■ About 15 muffins

3¼ cups (7½dl) all-purpose flour

⅔ cup (1½dl) sugar

4 teaspoons baking powder

2 teaspoons ground cardamom

1 pinch of salt

10 tablespoons (150g) butter, chilled and cut into small cubes

1 egg

1¼ cups (3dl) milk

FILLING

¼ cup (50g) softened butter

1 tablespoon vanilla sugar

2 tablespoons granulated sugar, divided

1 apple

1½–2 tablespoons freshly ground cardamom

¾ cup (115g) hazelnuts

1 egg, beaten

1. Preheat the oven to 450°F (225°C). Stir together the flour, sugar, baking powder, cardamom, and salt in a bowl. Add the butter and use your fingers or a food processor to make a crumbly mix. Add the egg and the milk and combine to make a firm batter.

2. Line a muffin pan with large muffin liners (preferably place two liners in one, so they become extra stable). Fill ¾ full with the batter.

3. To make the filling, mix the butter, vanilla sugar, and 1 tablespoon of the granulated sugar. Peel, core, and cut the apple into thin slices. In a separate bowl, mix the cardamom and the remaining 1 tablespoon of granulated sugar. Make a small indentation in each of the muffins and insert an apple slice, a little cardamom sugar, and a dollop of the butter mixture, about 1 teaspoon. Reserve some cardamom sugar to sprinkle over the muffin tops.

4. Coarsely chop the hazelnuts. Brush the top of the muffins with the beaten egg and sprinkle them with the rest of the cardamom sugar and the hazelnuts. Bake the muffins on the middle rack of the oven for 20–25 minutes, or until the muffins feel set and start to get a nice golden-brown color. Let the muffins cool a little, under a clean dishcloth, and serve them right away—while they're still warm—with some fresh butter, if you like.

ALTERNATIVE FILLINGS

* Apple and cinnamon
* Apple and almond paste mixed with butter and sugar
* Blueberries and butter flavored with sugar and vanilla
* Banana and chocolate

COCONUT WAFFLES WITH HONEY

If you have any left over, these waffles are the perfect thing to have for a snack or picnic. They're such a treat we have them for dessert sometimes. Just reheat the waffles in the oven at 200°F (100°C) and serve them with a dollop of your favorite ice cream—or enjoy them cold with butter, as my dear grandmother Wivi did. And of course they're divine hot, with a drizzle of fresh honey.

15 minutes ▪ About 12 waffles

2 eggs

1¾ cups (4dl) flour

1 14-ounce can (400g; 4dl) coconut milk

4 teaspoons baking powder

½ teaspoon salt

1 tablespoon fresh honey, ideally organic and locally sourced

5 tablespoons (75g) melted butter

2 ripe mashed bananas

½ cup (1 dl) toasted coconut flakes

Butter to grease the waffle iron

FOR SERVING

Fresh honey, for drizzling

Toasted coconut chips (optional)

Sliced banana (optional)

Scoop of ice cream (optional)

1. Separate the egg whites and yolks into 2 separate bowls. Beat the egg whites until they're light, fluffy, and form peaks. Set them aside. In the other bowl, mix the egg yolks with the flour, coconut milk, baking powder, salt, honey, melted butter, bananas, and coconut flakes. Let the batter rest for about 30 minutes and then fold the egg whites into the batter.

2. Add a dollop of butter to the surface of a preheated waffle iron and then pour in about ⅓ cup (about 1 dl) of the batter. Cook each waffle for 4–5 minutes or so, until it's crisp and golden brown. Repeat the process until the batter is gone.

3. Serve the waffles immediately with a drizzle of honey and a sprinkle of toasted coconut. If you like, add a few banana slices or a scoop of your favorite ice cream to the top.

HONEY COOKIES
WITH LEMON

You can easily prepare and quickly bake a lot of these chewy and slightly caramel-like cookies.

30 minutes ■ 36 cookies

10 tablespoons (150g) softened butter

⅔ cup (1½dl) sugar

2 tablespoons honey

2 tablespoons fresh lemon juice

Grated zest of 1 lemon

1¾ cups (4dl) flour

1 teaspoon baking soda

1 tablespoon vanilla sugar

1. Preheat the oven to 400°F (200°C). Line baking sheets with parchment paper.

2. Beat the butter, sugar, and honey in the bowl of an electric mixer until smooth. Add the lemon juice and zest. Mix the flour, baking soda, and vanilla sugar into the batter and stir to combine thoroughly. Work the mixture with your hands to form a dough.

3. Shape the dough into walnut-size balls and drop them lightly onto the lined baking sheets. Flatten the balls gently with your fingers. Bake the cookies on the middle rack of the oven for about 10 minutes or until the cookies turn light golden brown on the bottom (gently lift the cookies to check for doneness).

NOTE The lovely thing about honey is that it tastes as good for you as it is good. The antibacterial and immune-supportive properties of honey make it a super-healthy addition to tea during the cold season. But do be aware that the beneficial properties of honey deteriorate if it is heated too much.

DELUXE PANNA COTTA

It may sound redundant to call this smooth, creamy, decadent dessert *deluxe*, but that's exactly what it is. The secret lies in boiling down half the cream, which yields a flavor and texture that is out of this world. Fresh berries are hard to come by in the winter, but thawed frozen berries make a delicious topping with a little honey and, if you can find it, a couple of tablespoons of elderflower syrup. If you buy the syrup online or at a gourmet food store, you'll be surprised by how often you use it to flavor many other things. Try it in herbal teas, sodas, lemonade, cocktails (the grapefruit notes in the sweet syrup pair nicely with gin), and champagne. If you want to serve this lovely dessert to guests, be sure to factor in about 4 hours of fridge time.

about 45 minutes + 4 hours in the fridge ▪ 4 servings

3½ cups (8dl) heavy cream, divided

1 vanilla bean, seeds scraped out

2 tablespoons sugar

1 packet (7g) unflavored gelatin

TOPPING

2 tablespoons honey

2 tablespoons elderflower syrup

½ cup (50g) mixed fresh or frozen berries, thawed

1. Pour half the cream into a wide, heavy-bottomed saucepan over medium heat, and let it boil down to a little more than 1 cup (2½dl). Stir occasionally so the cream does not burn. Pour the hot cream through a fine sieve into a large bowl.

2. Stir the vanilla seeds and the bean into the reduced cream with the sugar and the rest of the cream. Bring the mixture to a boil and stir until the sugar is completely dissolved. Remove the pan from the heat, and sprinkle the gelatin over the surface of the warm cream. Stir until the gelatin has melted.

3. Let the mixture rest for about 20 minutes and then remove the vanilla bean. Pour the mixture into four bowls, cover them with plastic wrap, and refrigerate them for at least 4 hours.

4. To make the topping, gently heat the honey in a small saucepan with the elderberry syrup until the mixture liquefies. Fold the berries into the honey mixture and gently mix them in. Top the bowls of panna cotta with the berries

FLAVORINGS

This chapter is a bit of a catchall and includes some of my favorite recipes for little extras that add a burst of flavor, richness, spiciness, brininess, smoke, or zing to the table, including some that accent wintertime grilling, either outside, over coals or wood, or inside, on the stove top. Other recipes for accompaniments like Green Chili Slaw bring a little taste of sunshine to the plate when it's cold outside, and flavored butters add interest to hearty dishes, from casseroles to baked potatoes and roasted veggies. Have fun with these recipes and don't be afraid to improvise.

HOMEMADE RICOTTA

I use ricotta in lasagnas, gratins, desserts, and pizzas and mix it with eggs and Parmesan cheese to make extra-rich casseroles. Ricotta is easy to make, and if you have milk that's getting a little old, it'll perfect for this recipe.

30 minutes + 2–3 hours in the refrigerator

■

1¾ cups (4dl) ricotta

4 quarts (4 liters) milk
⅔ cup (1½dl) heavy cream
1 small pinch of salt
1 tablespoon lemon juice or vinegar

1. Mix the milk, cream, and salt in a large pot and heat it over low heat until the mixture reaches 175°F (80°C). Stir it every now and then, so that it doesn't burn on the bottom. Add the lemon juice or vinegar, reduce the heat, and continue to stir until the mixture starts to separate into curds. This takes about 2 minutes. It's very important not to boil the mixture. Remove the pot from the heat and let it cool, covered.
2. Pour the mixture into a cheesecloth (or a really clean kitchen towel or a coffee filter) set over a large bowl, and allow it to drain, preferably for 2–3 hours in the refrigerator. Every so often, discard the liquid (the whey) that collects in the bowl. The longer you drain the ricotta, the thicker the ricotta. Transfer the ricotta to a clean jar with a secure lid and store it in the refrigerator, where it will last up to about 10 days.

HOMEMADE BUTTER

There is butter and then there is *butter*. I've learned one true thing about making butter: the better the cream, the better the butter. In my village in Sweden, we have the luxury of buying milk and cream from an organic dairy farm, which makes all the difference—and it's easy and fun to make your own butter, especially if you have children who want to help in the kitchen.

25 minutes   ■   8 ounces (250g) butter

1 quart (1 liter) whipping cream
Olive oil
Flaked salt

1. Whip the cream in the bowl of an electric mixer until it starts to become granular and has formed both liquid (buttermilk) and small lumps of butter. Whip a bit more carefully toward the end so the liquid doesn't splash and the lumps don´t fly out of the bowl. This takes about 3 minutes. Strain the buttermilk (store it and use it for other recipes or drink it right on the spot!), and return the butter to the bowl.
2. Rinse the butter by pouring ice water over it and pressing the remaining buttermilk out with a wooden spoon or your fingers. Pour off the water and repeat the process. Keep rinsing and squishing the butter with the ice water until the water runs clear. You'll probably need to change the water three times.
3. Knead the butter with a wooden spoon and add a few tablespoons of good olive oil (for both flavor and texture) and some flaked salt, according to preference and taste. Transfer the butter to a clean jar with a snug lid and keep it refrigerated.

SALSICCIA BUTTER

The fennel in the sausage, and the garlic and sage make this butter extra delicious on just about anything, whether it's a baked potato or a crusty loaf of country bread. It is wonderfully versatile, so try it in savory recipes that call for "regular" butter.

25 minutes + at least 1 hour in refrigerator

■

About 12 ounces (350g) butter, 8 servings

 5 ounces (150g) raw, fresh salsiccia (sweet Italian fennel) sausage
 3 large cloves of garlic
   Oil for frying
 10 sage leaves
 1¾ sticks (200g) softened butter
   Juice of ½ lemon + zest of 1 lemon
   Salt and freshly ground black pepper

1. Remove the skin from the sausage and chop it finely. Slice the garlic thinly. Pour a little oil into a frying pan and fry the meat until it almost cooked through. Add the garlic and sage and continue to fry until the garlic is soft and the meat is completely cooked through. Let the mixture cool completely.
2. Blend the meat mixture with the butter, lemon juice, and lemon zest in a food processor or blender. Season with salt and pepper. Spoon the butter onto a sheet of parchment paper and roll it up into a tight sausage shape. Refrigerate the butter for at least 1 hour before serving. If you want to store the butter longer, it will keep for about 1 month in the freezer. Just remember to take it out well before you intend to serve it, so that it has time to reach room temperature.

YOGURT SAUCE WITH SCALLIONS AND APPLE

This sauce manages to be sweet, tart, hot, creamy, and refreshing all at the same time. It is particularly delicious with grilled meats and fish.

10 minutes + 1 hour in refrigerator ■ **4 servings**

 3 scallions
 1 large clove of garlic
 ½ tart, crunchy apple, such as Granny Smith, peeled
 ½ green chile pepper (or jalapeño), seeded
 2 tablespoons mayonnaise
 7 ounces (2dl) plain Greek yogurt
   Salt and freshly ground black pepper

1. Roughly chop the scallions, garlic, apple, and chile. Transfer the chopped ingredients to a bowl and add the mayonnaise and ⅓ the yogurt. Mix to combine all the ingredients. Stir in the rest of the yogurt and season with salt and pepper.
2. Refrigerate the sauce for at least 1 hour before serving, especially if it has become a little runny.

OPPOSITE: Yogurt Sauce with Scallions and Apple (top), The Vicarage House Rub, recipe on page 200 (right), Salsiccia Butter (bottom)

THE VICARAGE HOUSE RUB

I have the good fortune to live with my family in an old vicarage on the west coast of Sweden. We do a lot of grilling in the summer and have found that this rub is particularly versatile and so delicious that we use it year-round.

30 minutes ▪ 1 large jar

2 teaspoons fennel seeds

2 teaspoons whole cumin seeds

2 teaspoons coriander seeds

2 teaspoons yellow mustard seeds

1 whole dried peperoncino chile (piri piri), or about ½ teaspoon red chile flakes

1 star anise

2 teaspoons onion powder

1 tablespoon paprika

1 tablespoon smoked paprika

2 teaspoons salt

1 teaspoon freshly ground, coarse black pepper

2 tablespoons brown sugar

1. Toast the fennel seeds, cumin seeds, coriander seeds, mustard seeds, peperoncino, and star anise in a hot, dry pan until the spices sizzle. Let them cool slightly and then grind them in a spice grinder. (A mortar and pestle works equally well.)
2. Thoroughly mix the ground ingredients with the onion powder, both kinds of paprika, salt, pepper, and brown sugar. Transfer the mix to a jar with an airtight lid. Store the rub in a dry, dark place and it will keep 2–3 months.

PICKLED CABBAGE

It takes no time at all to whip together this recipe for pickled cabbage. It is particularly good with roast pork.

15–20 minutes ▪ 4–6 servings

2 cups (½ liter) water

1 tablespoon cider vinegar

½ teaspoon superfine sugar

2 teaspoons salt

½ head (6–8 leaves) purple cabbage

1. Bring the water, vinegar, sugar, and salt to a boil in a large pot. Break off the cabbage leaves, add them to the pot, and simmer over medium heat until the cabbage is soft but still has a little firmness in the thicker portions of the leaves. This takes about 10 minutes. Remove the mixture from the heat. Serve the pickled cabbage warm or refrigerate and enjoy it cold.

QUICK-PICKLED RED ONION

It's surprising how little time it takes to pickle onions—and the result is so good. Try it with BBQ brisket or really anything that comes off the grill.

35 minutes ▪ 4 servings

1 large red onion
Juice of 1 large lime
1 pinch of salt

1. Slice the onion finely and place in a bowl. Add the lime juice and press it gently into the onions with the back of a spoon until they becomes a little soft. Add the salt and let the onion mixture rest for about 30 minutes before serving.

GREEN CHILI SLAW

This slaw is unbeatably good with BBQ and burgers. It will wake up your taste buds any time of the year, so don't think you can't make it in the middle of winter to go with just about any meat or fish your roast or grill indoors.

20 minutes + 30 minutes ▪ 4 servings

1 medium head (500g) white cabbage (or a combination of red and white cabbage)
1 yellow onion
1–2 jalapeños, seeded
½ cup (25g) chopped cilantro
2-inch piece (25g) fresh ginger
1 large clove garlic, finely chopped
4–5 tablespoons lime juice
1½ tablespoons brown sugar
1½ tablespoon fish sauce
¼ cup (½dl) mayonnaise
Salt (optional)

1. Slice the cabbage finely with a mandoline or sharp knife. Slice the onion thinly, and finely chop the chile. Mix together along with the cilantro in a large bowl.
2. Peel and finely chop or grate the ginger. Mix the ginger, garlic, lime juice, brown sugar, and fish sauce with the cabbage mixture. Massage the slaw, preferably with your hands, to tenderize the cabbage. Mix the mayonnaise into the cabbage and let it rest for 30 minutes. Add a little salt, if you like, and serve.

ASIAN PICKLED FENNEL

This is supergood with chicken and fish, and perfect as a garnish for an Asian-inspired omelet.

25 minutes ▪ 2 small jars

1 cup (2½ dl) water

½ cup (1¼ dl) rice wine vinegar

½ cup (1 dl) sugar

1½ tablespoon salt

2 bulbs of fennel

1 Thai chile pepper or other type of chile

1. Bring the water, vinegar, sugar, and salt to a boil in a pot. Cut away the upper parts of the fennel so that bulbs are about the same size. Halve the fennel bulbs through the core, remove the core, and then thinly slice the bulbs. Slice the chile and then place it, together with the fennel, in a scrupulously clean glass jar and add the hot-water mixture.

2. Let the mixture cool and then put on the lid. Serve the pickled fennel immediately or store it in the fridge. If the jar has been properly sterilized, the fennel should keep for several months.

DIY BACON

If it's not too cold outside to use your smoker, you can invest a week and cure your own bacon and use it during the winter. It's easy and amazingly tasty. Just be sure to get a good piece of pork from your butcher.

About 40 rashers of bacon

2 chipotle chiles

4 cloves garlic

½ cup (1 dl) salt

2 tablespoons granulated sugar

½ teaspoon saltpeter (available online if you can't source locally)

1¾ pounds (800g) fresh pork belly

2 tablespoons coarsely ground black pepper

1. Roast the chiles in a dry frying pan and then grind them. Crush the garlic cloves. Mix together the salt, sugar, and saltpeter and rub it into the meat. Then thoroughly massage the meat with the garlic, ground chiles, and black pepper. Place the meat in a heavy plastic bag and refrigerate it for 1 week.

2. Remove the meat and let it come to room temperature. Smoke the meat over hickory chips at 200°F (100°C) until the bacon has an internal temperature of about 150°F (65°C). Allow the bacon to cool and then, using a meat slicer, cut it into thin pieces. Enjoy!

BADASS BBQ SAUCE

A really good BBQ sauce can be used with all kinds of grilled meat. This one has a lovely sweetness and kick that works nicely as both a sauce and a glaze. It's wonderful for classic BBQ dishes, beer-can chicken, brisket, and ribs—and of course you can use it during the wintertime, when outdoor cooking just isn't an option, for meat roasted in the oven or prepared in a grill pan on the stop top.

20 minutes ▪ About 2 cups (5dl)

3 inch piece (50g) of fresh ginger

1 large yellow onion

2 cloves of garlic

1 tablespoon whole yellow mustard seeds

1 whole chipotle chile

Oil for frying

½ cup (1 dl) apple cider vinegar

2 (400g) tart, crisp apples, such a Macoun, Granny Smith, or Gravenstein

½ cup (1 dl) cane sugar

¾ cup (2dl) hoisin sauce

½ cup (1 dl) ketchup

Salt and freshly ground black pepper

1. Peel and finely chop the ginger, onion, and garlic. Sauté with the mustard seeds and the whole chipotle in a saucepan with a little oil until the onion is soft. Add the vinegar and bring the mixture to a boil. Peel, core, and dice the apples. Stir them, together with the cane sugar, hoisin sauce, and ketchup, into the pan.

2. Bring the mixture to a boil and cook covered for 10–15 minutes or until the sauce has cooked down by half. Stir it every now and then. Season the sauce with salt and pepper. Pour the sauce into a blender and process until it is silky smooth.

3. Pour the sauce into a clean jar and put on a lid. You can serve the sauce warm or cold—it's delicious either way, and will keep for at least 2–3 weeks in the refrigerator.

PICKLED BEETS

15 minutes + 50 minutes ▪ **6–8 servings**

1 pound (500g) beets, cleaned and stems removed

½ cup (1¼dl) good white wine vinegar or sherry vinegar

¾ cup (2dl) sugar

1⅓ cup (2½dl) water

1 tablespoon salt

10 white pepper corns (whole)

10 whole cloves

1¼-inch piece (3cm) fresh horseradish, cut into slices

Wash and scrub the beets until they are completely clean. Boil them in salted water until the beets are tender (about 20–50 minutes, depending on size) and then rinse them. If the beets are very small (the size of a golf ball), it´s nice to pickle them whole, but if not, you can cut them either into slices or small wedges. Put the beets into a large, clean glass jar (see Note below). Add the remaining ingredients to a stockpot and bring the mixture to a rapid boil. Pour the hot pickling liquid over the beets so they are completely submerged and the liquid comes to within an inch of the top of the jar. Seal the jar with a lid. The beets can be kept in either the fridge or pantry and will last for at least six months, as long as the jar and lid have been properly sterilized.

> **NOTE** To properly sterilize jars for use, wash jars and the lids thoroughly and place them in a preheated oven at 212°F (100°C) for 30 minutes.

INDEX

ACKNOWLEDGMENTS

Marcus, Lilly, and Hjalmar, my greatest loves, thank you for always coming to my wildest ideas with support, enthusiasm, and a "we'll figure it out" attitude, while staying hungry, ready to pitch in, and always ready to laugh. We are the world's best super-team!

My beloved family in Skillingaryd, Sjötofta, and Falkenberg, thanks for all the support, all the incredible help and assistance with everything from administrative organization and packing to babysitting and cardiopulmonary resuscitation in the backyard! And special thanks for the good food (in our family, we are always ready to have a little something).

Magnus Carlsson, super awesome photographer, friend, and neighbor. I'm so happy and thankful that you are right on the other side of the cow pasture and share your beautiful images with the world. Your fine whistling, bad jokes, and slick ballet poses—just icing on the cake!

The world's best editor, Annika Ström, thanks for your well-trained eagle eyes, your eternal patience, infectious laughter, and last but not least, your big heart!

Super publisher Kerstin Bergfors, thank you for your trust, cheerleading, professional intuition, and excellent movie tips.

To the consummate marketer Ulla Joneby, my greatest advocate in publishing, who ensures that my cookbooks find a home abroad, I have no idea how you do it, but you are really phenomenal. Thank you!

Thanks to all the warm, happy, and super-professional staff at Bonnier Fakta, for always making it incredibly fun to step inside the doors at Sveavägen 56.

To all the incredibly talented, local food manufacturers in Halland—thank you for inspiring me more than I can say. For your work and sweat, you deserve the biggest gold star ever. Keep doing wonders!

Thanks to my village—Skrea Backe, a paradise on earth, the finest place to live and work, where I'm surrounded by the best neighbors in the world and the knowledge that I could survive for a very long time solely on the good in our village.

All friends, near and dear, thank you for your support and inspiration!

And most important of all, thanks to all you readers and followers who are buying my books, watching my TV-shows, cooking my recipes. You inspire me!

ABOUT THE AUTHOR

Lisa Lemke is a food consultant, recipe developer, food stylist, and television chef. She writes about food for various media, including magazines, books, radio, television, and advertising. She is the author of *The Summer Table* (Sterling Epicure), and one of the hosts of *Kitchen Dinners* on TV4. Lisa lives in the countryside in an old vicarage on the west coast of Sweden with her husband Marcus Nordgren, also a chef, and their two small children. Lisa and Marcus recently opened a pizzeria on their property, Prostens Pizza, which features local products and has become a huge success, with visitors coming from all over the country.